ADDITIONAL PRAISE FOR

Permanent Marker

"In *Permanent Marker,* Aimee Ross doesn't shy away from telling the hard truths of tragedy. She explores her own, personal trauma with raw honesty from her newly recharged heart while searching for that trauma's meaning with a candid, conversational style. Aimee's story reminds us that even when our truths don't reveal themselves in the ways we wish they would, we can always choose how those truths shape, rather than define, our lives."

Darin Strauss
Bestselling author of *Half a Life: A Memoir*

"In a series of tragedies that would be unbelievable in fiction, everything is broken—Aimee Ross's marriage, her heart, and finally, her whole body, tooth to toe. A devastating car accident could have been the end of her story, but Ross possesses an indomitable spirit and fierce humor that breathe new life into every page. Clear-eyed and open-hearted, Ross throws open the curtain to her hospital room, revisiting the harrowing, daily details of her trauma and recovery, writing herself to wholeness, and reminding us all of the crucial difference between merely surviving and making a decision to live."

Jill Christman
Author of *Darkroom: A Family Exposure* and *Borrowed Babies: Apprenticing for Motherhood*

"Filled with brutal honesty, heartbreak and humor, Aimee Ross's gut-wrenching story is an inspiring portrait of strength and resilience. Aimee, a truly gifted, creative, and award-winning high school teacher, discovers that it was her students who help her abandon her fears, renew her passion for teaching, and find the joy and meaning in her spared life...sharing a lesson that can help any one of us in our personal or professional life."

Debra Hurst
2016 National Teachers Hall of Fame Inductee

"Aimee Ross spares no details in her raw, unflinching account of what it means to have your life torn apart—physically and emotionally. *Permanent Marker* is a remarkable story of healing, courage, and finding the strength it takes to rewrite your life's story."

Tina Neidlein
Humor writer and author of
The Girl's Guide and *It's a Mom Thing*

"Aimee Ross sees the patterns of literature weaving through life. So when she is slammed with catastrophes that shatter her body and threaten her soul, she finds signposts to recovery through foreshadowing, symbols and yes, irony—which makes hers not just a resurrection story, but one laced with laughs."

Jan Shoemaker
Author of *Flesh and Stones: Field Notes from a Finite World*

Sept. '18

PERMANENT MARKER

A Memoir

• • •

AIMEE ROSS

*For Kristiane —
Another book lover!*

Aimee

KiCam
PROJECTS

A version of "August 2012" first appeared as the essay "Permanent Marker" in *Scars: An Anthology* (Wood, Et Alia Press, 2015).

A version of part of "March-May 2010" first appeared as the essay "Crossing" on SixHens.com (Issue 4).

Cover and book design by Mark Sullivan

ISBN 978-0-9991581-0-4 (paperback)
ISBN 978-0-9991581-1-1 (e-book)

Printed in the United States of America

Published by KiCam Projects
www.KiCamProjects.com

For Jackson,
who believed in me
before I believed in me

The Trifecta of Shit.

That's how I like to refer to it.

The end of my marriage. My own heart attack. An under-the-influence driver on a collision course to destroy the life I had just started to rebuild.

And all within six months.

The Triple Crown. A trio. Isn't the third time the charm?

Heart, body, soul: I was marked.

But I couldn't let—scratch that—I *wouldn't* let the Trifecta define my life.

"Only after disaster can we be resurrected."

~Chuck Palahniuk, *Fight Club*

August 2012

x x x x x x x x x x x x x x x x x x x x ◆ ◆

I stood naked on a wooden box in the meat-locker cold of the plastic surgery prep room, where two nurses watched as the surgeon marked my body with a black Sharpie.

He sat on a stool, eye level with my abdomen, leaning forward, drawing slowly. He paused, rolling the stool backward with his heels, and took in the surgical map of my front in its entirety.

I was freezing, and self-consciously I wondered if he had noticed my nipples, erect from the cold. If he had, he wasn't showing it. Instead, he moved forward again and resumed the process of grabbing skin, charting lines, and scrutinizing the results. He took his time, but it was okay. I wanted him to go slowly. I wanted him to make sure the markings were perfectly placed.

In just minutes, he would be cutting those lines and "revising" the scar that ran the length of my torso—the scar made to save my life two years before.

Actually, there were more than ten scars all over my body from that night. Places where bones punctured skin and chest tubes inflated lungs. Where a seatbelt held me fast. Where crushed, sharp metal scored skin. Where an eight-inch plate braced a snapped humerus and a three-inch pin secured a fractured pelvis. Where wires and screws held a dislocated foot in place. Where IVs found the perfect veins to tap.

Some of the scars were short, some were long, some were hard to see—but almost all of them were vertical.

At right angles to a horizontal plane. Perpendicular. The same angle at which we collided when he ran that stop sign and into my car, T-boning it and me. My vertical scars, the places I was put back together, stitched back up.

And none of them compared to the disfiguring scar running the length of my abdomen. The scar I worried people could see through my clothing. The scar that hurt to the touch.

I hated this fucking scar.

"Should I try to save your belly button?" the surgeon asked, pulling the permanent marker away from my flesh and looking up just long enough to speak.

I was surprised by the option. No one would even consider it a navel as it was, smashed up and pushed away from its point of origin.

"No, it's okay."

Two years before, trauma doctors had not asked me what to save. They had not planned the carved path their knives would take, nor did they plot the route around my belly button. They were trying to save my life. They just cut.

"We had to have them do *that*," my brother once said, pointing to my abdomen, "to be able to have you here now."

That.

I could almost picture *it*. Me, unconscious and naked, blue paper medical drapes covering legs and arms, breasts and belly exposed. Me, flat on a stainless-steel table in a cold operating room, where white lights radiated and whispery instructions intensified. A quick surgical cut, the flash of blade piercing flesh, just above the sternum down, down, down around the umbilicus, down still farther to the pubis.

Done. That quick. A way to get inside.

Internal bleeding, lacerated organs, a ruptured spleen. My body left open for the bleeding to stop, the swelling to lessen. Closure of muscle tissue only, a wound vac in place until the outside could be surgically pulled together.

But I didn't want *that* surgery, so the vacuum stayed in—for almost three months.

Maybe I *should* have gone back under the knife. Maybe it was my fault.

This monstrous scar, gaping, was still tender two years later. I thought about the accident every time I got dressed. I cried every time I saw myself naked.

Doctors assured me the wound would grow together on its own, but no one could tell me what it would look like. I imagined a normal, smooth surgical scar. Surely, I believed, since they had cut me straight, my belly would mend together that way, too.

I was wrong.

When the skin of my abdomen finally had closed three months later, a messy, uneven, and ugly scar ran its length: a ten-inch-long ribbon undulating from just above my ribcage to just above my pubic bone. Thick, new pink skin stretched wide like a yawn and bridged the fingertip-deep crevice to smooth the fault line of my abdomen's landscape. The ruched tissue puckered in places and pulled in others, dividing my stomach, splitting subcutaneous fat, then narrowed to semi-thick closures at both ends.

Wow—such a poetic description, Aimee. And what bullshit.

The scar made me look as if I had another ass, but this one was in front. I still had my belly button, but it had been pushed to the side, forgotten. The entire area still hurt to the touch; the tissue of my abdomen had been bruised that deeply. My clothes even fit differ-ently. I shopped for maternity tops—twelve years after my last child was born.

I fucking hated it.

The plastic surgeon drew huge circles on my flanks, what he called the areas of skin just under the ribs and above the waist, where he would also perform liposuction. Then he traced dotted vertical lines around the scar and my smashed-up navel, along with another line, horizontal this time, from hipbone to hipbone.

This was for the tummy tuck—another scar to add to the canvas.

After he finished with his magic marker, I stepped down from the box, turned, and looked in the mirror, avoiding his and the nurses' eyes. I had never been completely naked in front of this many people before—at least not awake—and with each minute that passed in the cold, I became more embarrassed by my nudity. All of my flaws had been highlighted by a map of black ink stretching across the flesh of my abdomen, and somehow, I understood this strange picture. The skin around my scar would be cut away, the rest pulled together, smoothed tight, and stitched closed. The "disfigurement" a psychologist had once noted would be corrected, the excess fat and extra skin discarded.

"Okay," the surgeon said, tucking the pen into his pocket and slapping the palms of his hands on his thighs. "It's time! I'll see you when you wake up."

He stood up and smiled.

"You'll be great, Aimee," he reassured me, and I knew in that moment that he was the one who would be great, not me.

Nonetheless, it *was* time.

I

Alice: "How long is forever?"

White Rabbit: "Sometimes, just one second."

~Lewis Carroll, *Alice's Adventures in Wonderland*

❋

❋

❋

❋

❋

❋

❋

❋

Two headlights in my left periphery. No time to react. An almost instantaneous blow, vehicle against vehicle. And then it all went black.

Or did it? I couldn't remember. *Time passed,* I thought.

How long?

Was that someone screaming? She's screaming at me. I raised my head and looked over at her. She asked if I was okay. I couldn't answer. I didn't know.

What I did know was that my front tooth had been knocked out. Cool air filled the gap that once held what I now felt laying on my tongue. It seemed much smaller than a front tooth should.

Who was that beside me, talking through the window?

"Ma'am, can you hear me?" someone asked. "Are you okay?

I lifted my head to answer him.

I don't know, I wanted to say, but nothing came out. I didn't know if I was okay, but my mouth wouldn't form words. My brain wouldn't let my voice respond. *Why couldn't I talk?*

"Ma'am?"

Jagged pieces of something white were coming out of my leg. Or was it my foot?

I saw it, even from the twisted angle of my seat. Bones coming through skin. Blood. Oh my God.

I knew there had been an accident that warm July evening. I knew I was driving. And I knew my front tooth was gone.

The girls. I had three members of the high school dance team I coached in the car with me. *Were they okay?*

"Who is this?" the voice outside the car asked.

Jorden answered behind me.

"That's Aimee Young. She's a teacher at Loudonville High School," she screamed. "She's had a heart attack before!"

She sounded frantic, but somehow I felt relief.

Where was Emily? She had been right beside me in the front passenger seat, but she wasn't now. *And what about Sarah?* She was sitting behind Emily. *Did she get out okay?*

Two silhouettes. One beside me, the other behind him. They wanted to free me from the wreckage. Two arms reached inside my window, and I tried to move my body to help, twisting my left shoulder toward whoever was at the open window.

And then I heard a voice from inside the car.

"Stop moving or you are going to die."

Who was it? Who said that?

I stopped moving.

I understood.

This was bad. Really bad.

They lifted me out of the wreckage and onto some kind of board. A large, white sheet was draped over the back window where Jorden had been.

Was she out of the car, too? Or were they going to get her?

Flat on my back. The night sky. A zillion stars. A head moved over my face like a shadow. Kenny, once my husband of eighteen years but now my ex-husband of one month.

What's he doing here? How did he know?

"Aimee, you'll be okay," he said. "I love you."

We had known each other since we were both seventeen, and his voice was familiar and comforting, but I couldn't answer him. I still couldn't speak. If he was saying I'd be okay, I must have looked okay. *Did he see that my front tooth was missing?* And just as suddenly as he had appeared, he was gone.

They were wheeling me somewhere, but I didn't know where I was. *Inside? A hallway?* Everything was happening so quickly—*a hospital?* Someone leaned in and told me she loved me. *Natalie.* She was in another car—*behind us? Had she seen it happen?* I thought she was crying.

They were moving me again, through doors—*outside?* A helicopter was there—*for me?* It was so loud. And maybe the back was open. That was where they were taking me? They pushed me in, still lying flat, and immediately I sensed that we had lifted off. *But wait—was the back still open? What if I fell out?*

Then everything went black.

A cold, bright room where I was at the center. Nothing around me, just the ceiling above. I couldn't move.

Like peering through a mummy's bandages with eyes not completely opened.

Everything squinty and blurred around the edges.

But I felt like I knew where I was. *This place made sense.*

People came and went. *Who were they?*

They spoke in hushed voices, occasionally looking over at me, whoever they were.

Ryan, my daughter Jerrica's boyfriend, was the first person I recognized. Jerr, who'd just turned eighteen, was here, too. So was my sixteen-year-old daughter, Natalie. *Wait—Jerrica?* I thought she went to North Carolina on vacation with her friend Taylor. *Where was Connor, my son?* He was only eleven, but school was still out for the summer, and his youth league baseball had been over for weeks...

My mom was here. She kept talking in my ear.

"Aimee, you're in the hospital."

Why was she yelling?

She handed me a notebook and pen. I tried to grasp the pen but couldn't. If I lowered my eyes, I saw my hand—barely—and it was swollen, almost unrecognizable.

"What happened?" I scrawled.

"You were in a car accident. You're going to be okay," Mom shouted, as if doing so would make me understand. As if it would make me "okay."

Now I remembered. *My tooth. The helicopter.*

We had been on our way home from dance camp. I was the one who wanted to commute. It would save money for the girls and for me, since Natalie was also on the squad. But she had driven Jerrica's car.

Thank God she wasn't with me. Thank God that car didn't hit her. Beside me, a small, stuffed lion moved into my line of vision. Jerr held it. On the other side, Nat had an elephant, maybe.

Ryan grinned at me. He cracked a joke, something about chardonnay and an IV. I gave him a slow "thumbs up." My mom wasn't smiling. And the girls seemed so far away.

I wanted to talk to them, but I couldn't. And my eyelids were so heavy.

• • •

How many hours passed? How many days?

A male voice, kind and encouraging, coaxed me awake.

"Aimee, I need you to wake up and breathe."

I heard him, and I turned my head, trying to see him. *Who was he?*

"That's it, Aimee. Breathe," he urged.

I heard him again, but I couldn't do what he asked. I couldn't stay awake.

And then sometime, he was back—*the next day? the next hour?*—explaining that it was time for me to breathe on my own. The tube going down my throat was coming out.

Wait a second. I hadn't been breathing on my own? And there's a tube down my throat? How bad was this?

"I need you to take a deep breath in, Aimee, and then blow out through your mouth," he explained. "It's probably going to make you cough. Are you ready?"

I nodded.

I breathed in as much as I could and blew, and he pulled the tube from somewhere deep down my throat. I coughed and then felt a kind of freedom. Breathing on my own again didn't feel any different, unless I did it too deeply—that hurt. He placed long, skinny tubes into my nostrils and around my ears.

"Oxygen, to help you breathe," he said.

Something was on my tongue. I could feel it now.

I lifted my hand motioning toward it, and a different voice said, "Don't talk."

I kept gesturing.

"Calm down, Aimee. Stop moving. And please don't try to talk. Calm down."

They didn't understand. It was my front tooth. I knew it was.

Finally, a nurse leaned in, and I opened my mouth.

"Oh, well, there's the tooth you lost," she said. "That happens."

Such an offhand, breezy remark about my front tooth, one so vital to my smile. But she didn't care. It wasn't important to her.

Why had no one noticed it before now? And how had I not choked on it?

The nurse reached over, picked the tooth off my tongue, and just like that, it was gone. But I couldn't see what she did with it. I bet she tossed it into the trash can. I bet she even thought, "Welp, she doesn't need this any longer."

But it was my tooth, not hers. And she didn't have the right to do that.

I was pissed.

As soon as she turned her back, I lifted my right arm and stuck up my middle finger. A salute in honor of my front tooth, now gone forever. And I didn't care who saw.

Immature and meaningless, but it was all I could do. And it was enough.

• • •

Sometime during the middle of the night, when no one had been in my room for a while, I could hear music. Were the nurses playing it at their station to comfort patients?

Michael Jackson's "Thriller."

Ohio State University band music. The Best Damn Band in the Land. I remembered. My college alma mater.

Now "Purple Rain." It's Prince.

The melodies echoed from some peripheral place, looping over and over and over before settling in my brain.

A fuzzy nothingness surrounded me. I felt like people I knew were outside my room wanting to talk to me, staring at me as if I were on display. I didn't see them, but I thought I heard their voices.

The music eventually faded away to nothing. Time faded away to nothing, too.

Silence.

A nurse visited and told me they hoped to move me out of the ICU soon.

I was in intensive care?

A dog barked outside of my room. A man spoke, probably a fireman or an EMT. I pushed the buzzer. I wanted to pet that dog, feel its warmth.

"Can the dog visit me?" I asked.

There was no dog. There never had been, the nurse said.

"What happened to the music?" I asked.

There was no music; there never had been.

"You're hallucinating, a side effect of the drug changes in your system," the nurse explained.

They were weaning me off heavy sedation to painkillers so I could be moved. A good thing, I thought—my body was doing what the doctors hoped—but it also meant being relocated and transferred to another bed.

The new place was much different than before, more cozy: dim lighting, warmth, and a curtain dividing the room.

Several nurses came into the room. Maybe four, maybe five. They gathered round, grasping edges of the sheets or blankets to move my deadweight body. Grunting, struggling, and maneuvering, they lifted me into a new trauma bed. I was attached to so many sensors that even the slightest movement set off a chain reaction of onomatopoeia.

Beepbeepbeepbeepbeepbeepbeep.

My new roommate, hidden behind that thin patterned material, was not happy with this. I heard great sighs of disgust from her corner.

I faded in and out of a sleep filled with scattered, strange moments and vivid, broken dreams.

The computer in my room turned on, revealing a program that projected over an entire wall. By simply blinking my eyes twice (much like double-clicking a mouse), I could choose a virtual escape that would separate my mind from my body's trauma. And like the rides at Disney World that sweep you over beaches, cliffs, or rainforests, I sailed through spectacular oceanfront landscapes for a time, comfortable and free, until a notice popped up that in order to continue, I would have to provide my credit card information or be billed.

I worried that the trip my brain had taken was adding another cost to what had to be an already huge medical bill. I also wondered what kind of place I was in. What kind of hospital offered virtual brain escapes?

Later, God came to me in the form of a woman. Ethereal and fairy-like, she was dark-haired and wearing a long, gauzy white dress. She comforted me and then became Clifford the Big Red Dog. Clifford comforted me, too.

The voices of various family members mingled in conversation just outside my room, and I overheard a surprise being organized in the hopes that I was being moved home soon. *Home? Did they even know what was wrong with me yet?* I was worried, anxious, even in such a dreamlike state. *How could I go home when I couldn't even move my body?*

I dreamt of my family leaving secret gifts all over the room for me to take home, much like when Santa visits sleeping children on Christmas Eve. Two new overstuffed armchairs took the place of the hospital's dismal plastic ones. A shiny, new white fridge sat against the wall. Fluffy, pastel-colored towels were stacked on a table where a beautiful floral arrangement had been placed. There was even a nice set of toiletries left for me at the foot of my bed.

I heard voices of family fighting with nurses about removing the gifts, which nurses said weren't fair to the other patients. Then I overheard plans for a parade at the hospital in my honor—since there could be no gifts. In my sleepy, dreamlike haze I thought about waking up to my very own parade, and I couldn't wait.

But I woke up to stark emptiness.

Had I imagined everything? Where was everyone? Why hadn't they come in to see me?

I heard familiar voices outside the room again. My brother Brian's wife, Laurie. Mom. *Did I hear Connor, too? When would they come in?* I thought it had been a week since the accident, and Connor hadn't come to visit yet. I missed my baby boy.

Just then, my bed began to shake. Someone was underneath it.

"Connor? Is that you? Stop that! Quit hiding and come here. Come see me."

Connor was playing tricks on me, but I was drowsy and didn't have the energy for games.

I continued to float in and out of sleep.

"You must have made up your mind," Kenny spat at me, his boyish good looks lost in an angry scowl.

He had thrown open the door and stomped into the bedroom where I stood in the adjoining bathroom's doorway, staring into the mirror, concentrating on tweezing my eyebrows. Jerrica, Natalie, and Connor were just outside, watching TV in the living room.

"What are you talking about?" I asked in a low voice.

The last few weeks had been tense. He knew I wasn't happy, and I knew I had to do something about it. I turned away from the mirror, took a few steps, and shut the door behind him so the kids didn't hear.

"You've been calling divorce lawyers," he said, throwing down a phone bill he'd printed at work, detailing calls made from my cell. "So then yeah, you must have made up your mind!"

Ah, the divorce lawyers. I had called only a couple—and within the past two days—trying to find out what the timeline and cost might be. Really, I was just gathering information. I wanted to know what I would be getting into *if* I decided to proceed.

After eighteen years of marriage, lately we spent more time apart than together. Affection had turned to antagonism, and I had become cynical, angry, sad, and looking for something Kenny wasn't giving. I was miserable, and I couldn't imagine he was any happier.

"Well?" he asked. "*Aimee?*"

This was the moment. The inevitable, monumental moment that I knew had probably been coming. I either told him now, or I continued to live this lie. I breathed in through my nose and held it, steeling myself.

"Okay then, Kenny. I want a divorce."

Breathe out.

"Well, that's just fuckin' great," he growled.

The words slid out of his mouth and into his T-shirt as he bent over, sitting down on the edge of the bed. He held his head in his hands while I just stood there, allowing what had just come spilling out to sink in.

He pulled his wedding ring from its finger. The triceps of his upper arm clenched tight under the cut-off sleeve of his shirt as he gripped the ring, and then he threw it. Hard. The gold band, no longer a precious metal, bounced off the wall. *Clink.* I flinched.

"Don't you love me anymore?"

Tears rolled down his round cheeks, but I might as well have been that wall.

"Yes, I love you," I said in a quiet voice. "But not the way that I should for a marriage to work."

I watched him consider this. Resignation.

He didn't argue. He knew, too. Maybe he even felt the same way.

"You're telling the fucking kids," he snarled. "If this is what you want, then you"—he pointed a finger at me—"will tell them."

I shouldn't have been surprised, but I was. He was pinning the end of a twenty-year relationship on me, rather than seeing it as something we were both a part of. It proved what I had felt for a long time: Our marriage was no partnership. And in that moment, I knew he wouldn't fight for me. I wasn't sure it would matter if he did.

Defeated, Kenny walked out of the room. I knew he would retreat to the basement where he spent most of his off-work time, escaping to a virtual world where grown men played war games chasing after and shooting each other. I went into the kitchen to busy myself with mindless tasks and wrap my mind around the last half-hour.

There was no relief and no weight lifted. And I had no idea how I should be feeling.

What would happen now?

After a while, he came upstairs, stomped into our bedroom, and shut the door. He was grieving; I was reeling.

I knew the marriage was officially broken.

An hour or so later, I heard the bedroom door's familiar squeak. All three kids and I were sprawled in different positions and places on the living room's new brown furniture, still watching TV. Their father burst into the room.

"Your mother has something she wants to tell you," Kenny said through gritted teeth.

Oh no. Not now.

I wasn't ready; this wasn't fair. Especially not right before sending them to bed.

I was appalled. These were his children!

Tears started to fill every one of the kids' eyes—they knew. There was no use trying to get around it. They were aware of the tension; they heard the fights.

Jerrica, Natalie, and Connor: the three most important people in my life.

I was about to devastate them and destroy our family, taking the blame alone.

In that moment, I hated Kenny. This was my punishment, his way to get back at me, and I would never forgive him for this. My ability to protect my children, to tell them on my terms, was being controlled by his manipulation.

I stood helpless in the middle of the room, warm from the blood flooding the skin of my cheeks and neck. The thumping in my ears, the sound of my beating heart, drowned out the noise of the TV. How could a heart beat when it was breaking?

"Tonight I told your father I wanted a divorce."

Nine words. Enough to break promises, enough to break a family.

I felt hollow. My heart, crushed in a single life-changing moment, had shattered into countless irretrievable pieces.

That moment disintegrated into a fragmented tableau of several more: Kenny, his face in his hands sobbing, on the couch with a bewildered Connor, also crying. Jerrica in the recliner, Natalie on the loveseat. Both girls looked from me to their father, faces searching for an explanation. Jerrica moved to sit beside Kenny, and he collapsed into her chest, sobbing loudly.

In the blur of that moment, watching my children fall apart before my eyes, I had no idea what to do. I felt like I had said enough, but Kenny wouldn't speak. He no longer mattered now. In fact, he and his passive-aggressive, childish ass could go to hell. Our children were what mattered, and they needed me.

I sat on the loveseat then, away from him, and wrapped my arm around Natalie. She fell against me, crying hard. No one spoke save the voices of a trashy MTV reality show, while minutes trickled into one another. The clock above the TV marked time, hands ticking along with the intermittent sniffles and broken sobs.

I did not cry. Instead I wondered what tomorrow would be like. If my children would hate me. How I would get through the school day. How Kenny would treat me when he got home from work.

I braced myself when I noticed the crying fading. I had to break this spell.

"It's time for bed, kids."

Jerrica, Natalie, and Connor quietly gave us both goodnight hugs and kisses and went to their rooms. I knew they would lie in their beds, still crying, awake for hours, probably angry with me.

This was all my fault, wasn't it?

Kenny walked into our bedroom and shut the door. After more than twenty years together, I knew what he was thinking.

I hope you're happy now.

But I wasn't.

I had just broken the hearts of all the people I loved. I had broken my own.

None of us would ever be the same again.

The gray, gauzy haze finally lifted, along with my eyelids. I was awake.

Mid-morning light streamed through the open blind slats of a window to my right.

Two vinyl chairs sat at the foot of my bed, one brick red, the other drab orange. On the wall behind them, a square whiteboard announced the names of my assigned doctor and nurse in neat, loopy handwriting. Above it, a wall-mounted TV, and to the left, a computer on wheels half-hidden by the thin blue curtain dividing the room. A tray table beside me, another computer on wheels behind my shoulder. To my right, an IV machine.

From my forty-five-degree hospital bed angle, I could see I was neatly tucked into my environment, my body a letter enveloped in the white hospital sheet, a blanket turned down at my waist. My left arm was in a thin blue sling at my side, the other comfortably resting with an IV. An oxygen tube was up my nose, while what seemed like a hundred other tubes were either going into or coming out of my body at various angles.

I felt stiff, statue-like and confined, and when a nurse arrived to check my vitals, I asked if she could remove the covers from my legs. As she peeled the covers down to my ankles, I saw a cast encasing my left leg from the knee down. I slid it out from under the covers to try to lift it, but it was so heavy.

"Could you please pick my leg up and put it on top of the covers?"

"Of course. Your pedicure is gorgeous—very summery," she said as she gently picked up my heel and set it down.

"Oh, thank you."

My toenails, a glossy, sparkling fuchsia, peeked out above the edge of the cast. I had polished them the day before dance camp started. Their perfection looked ridiculous now in this sterile, bluish environment, but seeing them somehow made me feel better.

I watched highway traffic edge toward what I recognized as the Cleveland skyline while I lay there, taking in my surroundings.

"Hi, Aimee?" a man in a white coat said as he came from behind the curtain, pushing it aside to make room. He introduced himself as the trauma doctor on rounds that morning.

"I'm here to explain the extent of your injuries, let you know what's happened to your body."

I could tell from the sling and cast and scratches that I was pretty beaten up, but I didn't know how badly.

"Do you remember what happened?" he asked gently.

"Yes, sorta."

"Your car was T-boned," he said. He gestured with his hands, placing the fingertips of his right into the palm of his left. "You took the brunt force of the collision, because impact was at the driver's-side front wheel.

"Both your left ankle and foot are broken. The bones of your midfoot actually punctured your skin when they were displaced."

So those were the bones I had seen.

He continued, pointing to the top of the cast, "There are three screws here and two wires here holding your foot together now."

"Your pelvis and tailbone were also fractured. We had to put a screw into your pelvic bone to hold it in place as it heals," he explained. He lifted my hospital gown a bit and gently turned me to show a small, stitched hole on the back of my left hip where a screw was now holding me together.

Whoa. *My pelvis was fractured? Broken?* I couldn't believe it. And at the same time, I wondered what it really meant. *How can a person even move with a broken pelvis? Would I be confined to bed?*

"You also had another compound fracture in your upper left arm," the doctor went on. "You can see here"—he pointed to a spot on my upper arm—"where the bone broke the skin."

But wait. It was only in a sling. *Don't all fractured bones need casts?*

"A metal plate was put into your arm to hold the bone together as it heals, and since you're stuck in bed for a while, you don't really need a cast," he said.

I wondered if the plate and those screws would remain in my body, or if they would eventually need to be removed. But I was too shocked to ask.

"Nine of your ribs are fractured and your sternum is cracked," the doctor continued.

That explained the pain I felt in my chest when I breathed.

"Those just have to heal over time."

So many fractured bones, so much breakage. I felt light-headed, almost dizzy. It was all so overwhelming.

"Your lungs were punctured, probably when your ribs broke," he said. "We had to insert chest tubes to inflate your lungs, but they'll come out when you're getting adequate oxygen on your own."

The tubes, also draining fluid from my lungs, tugged at the skin around them with even the slightest movement.

"You also had a lot of internal trauma to your abdomen, Aimee," the doctor said.

He paused, almost hesitated. Something serious was coming next. I could feel it.

"The airbag and seatbelt saved your life, but because of the force, there was still damage. You sustained lacerations to your liver, kidneys, and lower intestine—there was a lot of bleeding. We had to remove your spleen."

Internal trauma.

Internal bleeding.

No more spleen.

"Is that bad?"

Now was the time to know.

"Well, it is an organ of the body, which of course we never want to lose. Your spleen filters blood and helps fight bacteria in your body, but you can live without it," the doctor explained.

I looked down where a drainage tube snaked out from under my hospital gown into a container at the end of my bed. A watery red liquid was collecting, coming from somewhere inside my abdomen. Later, when the nurse checked my wounds, I saw that the tube was attached to the middle of a black sponge in my still-open body. From my vantage point, the sponge stretched lengthwise from just under my breasts to my pubic bone and across my entire abdomen, a width of about eight inches. A clear plastic film had been stretched over it and around a tube that was attached to a pump to remove excess fluid while increasing the blood flow needed to heal my body. The entire apparatus was called a wound vac.

There it was again. That familiar hollow feeling. My body, crushed in a single life-changing moment, seemed to have shattered into countless irretrievable pieces.

It was broken. *I* was broken.

From the inside out.

How could all of this have happened?

The doctor studied my chart for a few more minutes before he looked up, cocked his head to the side, and frowned slightly, pursing his lips.

"We think you're going to make it," he said.

And with that, he was gone, on to his next patient visit.

Make it?

They think *I'm going to ...* make *it? Could I still die?*

It had been almost a week since the accident, and I was out of the ICU. I was awake. I was connected to all kinds of machines.

How could I not "make it"?

I sat there alone in stunned silence, tears falling down my cheeks.

I think I always knew our marriage wouldn't make it.

That one day, I would walk away.

But I don't know how or when I knew. I just knew.

In my heart. In my gut. In the back of my mind.

I mean, I couldn't complain. My life as a wife and mother of three was a stable one, for the most part. My husband was not an alcoholic who spent his evenings at the local bar, and he wasn't abusive. He didn't gamble away our money, and he wasn't unfaithful to our marriage. He was a good father and a decent provider.

"Boy, from the outside looking in, you'd never know," an acquaintance had said to me a few days—maybe hours—after I told Kenny I wanted a divorce.

For a second, I wasn't sure what the woman was talking about. Then I saw her eyes, wide with shock, and it hit me, like a slap in the face, there in the middle of the grocery store.

She was talking about my marriage. *My* relationship.

I was stunned. Offended. *Who says that to someone?*

Appearances must have sketched my marriage as perfect, but it wasn't.

Our relationship had gotten lost in the woods of our youth. Over time, we learned to cling to the rotting branches of immaturity while stumbling over exposed roots on the trail of who was right and wrong. We traveled in circles, playing to the same roles, rather than appreciating each other as growing and changing human beings, and eventually, we were stranded, having left no crumbs to follow back.

You'd never know what? I wanted to grumble back at her in the produce aisle. *Know that we were lost?* Maybe we didn't either. *Or maybe it was me,* I wanted to say. *Maybe it's none of your business,* I should have said.

Instead, I shrugged my shoulders, an "Eh, whattaya gonna do?" gesture. I didn't care about her opinion enough to have a conversation, and I wasn't interested in feeding her rumor-mill curiosity. Still, I couldn't believe she had the nerve.

From the outside looking in, you'd never know.

No, probably not, but wasn't that the case with every marriage?

Marriage. What a joke.

I had become jaded, believing wedding vows had been created by society to bind people together for a plethora of reasons—cultural, biological, legal, religious, and more. People just couldn't be meant for only one person their entire adult life, because that went against nature. Plus, statistically, half of all marriages failed.

Why did people even bother?

But twenty-four years ago, I hadn't believed that. Back when I was a kid, innocent and idealistic. Back when I thought that love was the only ingredient necessary for a successful relationship.

We just weren't good together anymore, and we fought. A lot. We were stuck in a rut—same schedule, same friends, and same things over and over and over. I took care of the house and him and the kids. He took care of coaching and playing video games.

As time passed, a feeling of discontent grew inside me—like an ivy whose tendrils mature slowly, creeping and crawling over one another until they are tangled and knotted and wrapped so intricately around whatever is in their way, the vines and what they are overtaking cannot be parted unless the life force is severed. This malaise threatened the wall of my heart, already weakened by the twisting, strangling competition of heavy guilt. What a painful ache.

Guilt for wanting independence, guilt for being selfish. I wanted to be myself. I wanted to be happy again. I wanted more than what my marriage was. I wanted to be in love.

And I wasn't anymore. Had I ever been?

What did it feel like, being in love? I couldn't imagine, couldn't remember. And yet, I must have been once upon a time. I mean, I'm pretty sure I loved Kenny when we got married, *right*? But I had been a mere kid. Did I even understand what love was then?

No, from the outside looking in, you probably *would* never know.

And a façade of perfection wasn't enough to hide the truth any longer.

July 1998

⁕ ⋄ ⋄ ⋄ ⋄ ⋄ ⋄ ⋄ ⋄ ⋄ ⋄ ⋄ ⋄ ⋄ ⋄ ⋄ ⋄ × ⁕

From the outside looking in, I was living the perfect storybook life, married to my high school sweetheart and the mother of two little girls when I fell hopelessly in love—at first sight—with another man.

I was in the heart of Europe—Warsaw, Poland—on a Holocaust study tour with fifty other teachers from around the United States, my first overseas trip. Learning about the Holocaust both fascinated and disgusted me, and I knew that my time there and in Israel the couple of weeks following would better prepare me to teach about it. But I was out of my element. I hadn't been alone or just Aimee— not wife, mom, teacher—in several years. It was weird.

Every morning at about the same time, I heard the rousing chant of the object of my affection on MTV Europe—the only Polish channel I could understand. "Go, go, go! *Allez, allez, allez!*" he shouted and sang. I was enchanted.

Who was this beautiful man with the velvety voice and energetic dance moves?

Two weeks later, the song still echoing in my brain, I repeated the lyrics to an Israeli music store salesman to find out who it was that I had fallen in love with.

A smile immediately crossed his face in recognition.

"Aaahhh, Ricky Martin," he responded, handing me a compilation CD with "The Cup of Life" on it.

But then I returned home to real life, my third pregnancy, and teaching, and I forgot about Ricky.

6

Until February 24, 1999: the forty-first Grammy Awards. Ricky re-appeared out of nowhere from once upon a time: still beautiful, still energetic, and still singing the same catchy song. *Oh my God, it's him*, I thought, and I was quickly under his spell again, charmed once more by my European MTV crush.

Ricky Martin was perfection to me, visually and musically—a flawless, romantic, Latin hero—and he came to symbolize more than just the soundtrack of my first trip abroad or my first stab at true independence. Ricky gave me something to believe in—something I couldn't quite put my finger on, but something I longed for—and I couldn't get enough of him or his music, no matter the language it was in.

I've been in love with him ever since.

When Mom and Natalie came to visit after the doctor's morning rounds, I felt myself sink back into the bed, the tension in my body unwinding at the sight of them. Natalie walked over and took my hand.

"Aw, hi, Nat."

My beautiful red-haired girl. Tears filled my eyes, eventually spilling over. I hated for her to see me like this.

"Hi, Mom," she said in sing-song, an ornery grin on her face.

Though it was a hot August day, Natalie wore her usual T-shirt, jeans, and flip-flops. The scent of her was a familiar mix of then and now: toddler skin warmed by sunshine and clothing that hinted at the men's Old Spice sport deodorant she insisted on wearing.

I realized I still heard music playing. Prince again.

"Can you guys hear that music? Where's it coming from?"

Mom squinted and Natalie wrinkled her nose, both were puzzled, and then they looked at each other.

"It's real faint—shhhh."

After a few seconds, I asked, "Hear it?"

Mom walked over to stand beside me and started rubbing my arm.

"Aimee," she said, "there's no music playing."

"Yes, there is."

"Mom," Natalie said, "Grandma's right. There's no music."

But I could hear it.

"Well, could you please turn off the TV, then?"

Mom took the remote control that hung from a cord beside me and pushed the power button to show me it actually had been off. The TV flashed to life, and sound blared from the pillow-side speaker on my bed. She pressed the button again so I could see the TV turn off this time.

"So the TV wasn't on?"

"No, hon," Mom said.

"Well, what about that over there? I think they're watching me through that."

I pointed across the room to a screen attached to the wall behind my roommate's bed.

Mom never asked who I thought was watching me. She understood. She explained that it was a computer the nurses used to enter vital information.

"Would you like me to cover it?" Mom asked.

I nodded, and she pulled the curtain so that it hung just slightly over the screen—not enough to disturb my roommate, but enough to calm me down.

"Why didn't Dad come yesterday? I heard him outside my room, but he never came in."

"Dad flew home Sunday with your sister. This is Tuesday. He wasn't here yesterday," Mom said.

"Well, weren't you guys outside my room yesterday, discussing me staying here? I heard Laurie in the hall talking. She said this is the worst hospital ever and that I should be moved somewhere else." Laurie, my brother Brian's wife.

"No, Aimee. That didn't happen," Mom said.

I looked at her skeptically. I had heard everything.

"I wouldn't lie to you," Mom said gently.

"But you brought Connor, right? And he was in my room, under the bed and in the corner hiding from me. He wouldn't quit moving my bed."

Mom looked at me with pity, while Natalie stared at me with wide-eyed concern trying not to laugh.

"Aimee, none of those people were here yesterday, and none of that happened," Mom said.

"Then why was my bed moving?"

I was so confused.

Natalie sat down on the edge of the bed near my feet, causing the bed to move. Air started plumping the mattress around her vibrating the bed.

"See? I told you! That's what Connor was doing. He was messing with me all night!"

"Mom, that's just the bed pumping air to even out the mattress," Nat said. "The mattresses inflate and deflate automatically in all the ICU beds."

What was happening to me? A look of worry came over my mom's face.

"Am I going crazy?"

I started to cry. I was terrified.

"No, honey. Calm down," Mom said. "You are on very strong medication to control your pain. They had to wean you off even stronger drugs in ICU, so that you could be moved here."

Mom left to get my nurse, who explained that the visions and music I was experiencing were actually hallucinations. They were a common side effect of the painkiller Dilaudid, which was being given to me through my IV.

"Can I have something else instead?"

"Of course," the nurse said with a smile. "I'll talk to your doctor. You aren't getting as much as you were, but we can still see about other pain meds that won't make you feel crazy."

I didn't need to lose my mind right now. It was the only thing I had control of.

"Are the other girls okay?"

"They're all fine, Aimee," Mom responded right away. "Do you remember what happened?"

"A car sped through a stop sign and slammed into us on the way back from dance camp."

What if the girls were in worse condition than I was? I knew from what the doctor had said that the driver's side of the car had taken the brunt of the other car smashing into us, but I had no idea what had happened to everyone else. Jorden had been sitting behind me, Emily was in the front passenger seat, and Sarah was behind Emily in the rear passenger seat. I remembered Emily beside me and talking one minute, and then the next, she was gone.

"So what happened to them?"

"Emily had her nose broken in two places, and Jorden got a lot of cuts on her forehead—she needed stitches," Natalie said. She was on the dance team with all three girls, but Emily and Jorden were classmates of Nat's and about to start their junior year of high school.

"What about Sarah?" Sarah was going to be a sophomore.

"She's okay, Mom," Nat said. "She wasn't hurt."

"Wait—Emily's nose was broken in *two* places?" Emily was one of Natalie's closest friends.

"Well, it was broken in the wreck, probably from the airbag they think," Nat explained. "And then when Emily got home from the hospital, she passed out and fell down. That's how she broke it again."

"Oh, wow," I said.

I was relieved that the girls were okay, but I could feel tears forming behind my eyes. I wanted to see them. I wanted to *know* they were okay.

"Look at me," I said, my chin trembling. "My life is ruined."

I paused to get control of my emotions. I couldn't believe this had happened. I was furious thinking about it. I had no idea what kind of recovery awaited me or how long it would take, not to mention whether permanent damage had been done to my body. My injuries had been explained only the day before, by the doctor who'd said they *thought* I was going to "make it."

A car had shot out of the darkness and into us, leaving me barely able to move.

Someone else's horrible, tragic mistake.

Only five months after I suffered a heart attack caused by stress.

"I better not find out the driver of that car was drunk or high…" I threatened, my voice trailing off.

I never finished that thought, and no one responded.

• • •

Later, after Mom and Natalie left, my younger and only brother, Brian, visited.

Just a year apart in age, we had always been close. We shared the same friends, the same music, the same first cars, and at one point, the same apartment in college.

While we spent a few moments catching up about my injuries and how I was feeling, I noticed that Brian seemed more somber than usual.

"So, Aim, do you know why you're here?" Brian asked, sitting down in the chair at the foot of my bed.

Well, duh, I wanted to say. *Was he teasing me?*

"Of course I do."

I searched his face for a trace of a smile, but there wasn't one.

"Then tell me why," he said. He was serious.

"I was in a car accident..." I heard my voice rise a little, like I was asking a question.

I'd been in the hospital for a week and on the trauma floor for a few days. My injuries and the tubes and cast and sling made things pretty obvious, especially to me. *Why was he asking this?*

"Do you remember anything else?" he asked.

I described what I could from what little memory I had of the accident. I had seen lights and then felt immediate impact, harder than I've ever felt before. A man talked to me while he and others cut me out of the wreckage, and then I was laid flat and put into the back of a helicopter. Kenny was there.

"Do you remember being taken to the hospital?" Brian asked.

"You mean here? No, I just remember being put into a helicopter."

"They took you to Ashland first. Then they life-flighted you here," Brian said.

Life flight. The only people I ever heard about being life-flighted from car wrecks usually died.

"Has anyone told you anything else?" Brian asked.

He ducked his head and leaned in, looking at me intently. I was starting to get a little confused.

"No, no one has told me anything. Why?"

What else was there to know?

"The driver of the other car was a nineteen-year-old kid. He died, Aimee."

I looked out the hospital room's window to my right at the highway traffic. Time stopped, just as it had the night of the accident. Yet somehow, those distant cars, now blurry and out of focus, still crawled toward a watery Cleveland horizon. Oh no.

Brian handed me a tissue.

"Do I know him? Did I have him in school?" I whispered, my chin quivering.

I had been teaching for eighteen years at the same small school; it was a distinct possibility.

"I don't think so," Brian answered. "He's not from Loudonville." And then he said his name. "Zach Ryder?"

He was a real person. Saliva gathered in my mouth like I might throw up. Like I knew him.

But I didn't. I shook my head.

"No, I don't know him."

"That night—of the wreck—I was in the waiting room of intensive care, between your room and his," Brian said.

He explained that upon impact, the young man had been ejected through his car's open sunroof and onto the road.

"He was life-flighted, also. His parents and sister were there, too," Brian went on.

As this settled into my consciousness, the situation grew exponentially more profound. Someone died in the same accident I was in. Someone young who had parents. And a sister. A family. Maybe even a dog.

"I saw a doctor talking to them," Brian continued. "It was pretty obvious that he had died, because they all started to cry. I also heard someone mention organ donation."

"Oh, wow."

"Yeah," Brian agreed, "but get this."

He raised his eyebrows and shook his head, preparation for what came next.

"It couldn't have even been five minutes later. The father and sister walked across the room to me and apologized for what had happened. They both hugged me," Brian said. "They said they hoped you would be okay. I just couldn't believe it. It was so sad, and all I could do was thank them."

I swallowed and glanced down at my left foot. I remembered seeing bones. And blood.

And he was dead.

I didn't know what to say. I was horrified by the gravity of the entire situation, but I was still pissed. He did this to me, his car crushing my body, his driving putting me in a hospital bed.

"Aimee, you need to know one more thing," he continued. "The kid was driving a Mini-Cooper. You know what those are, right? How small they are?"

I nodded yes.

"If he'd have been driving anything other than that, *anything*, you would be dead, too. There's no doubt about it," he said.

I was lucky to be alive was what Brian was saying. Then he confirmed it.

"You're a miracle, Aimee."

February 2010 | Three Nights after "I Want a Divorce"

* *

There is no way I'm having a heart attack.

I'm only forty-one.

Panic attack, maybe.

Anxiety, I thought.

But that didn't explain the cement block lying across my chest or the five-ton elephant stepping on it. And it didn't explain the softball-sized knot under my ribcage or the profuse sweating. I felt like I could throw up at any second.

I knew someone had better take a look at me, so I drove myself to the hospital in a late winter snow storm. Alone.

(I know, I know. Bad idea, Aimee.)

While the ER nurse filled out admissions paperwork, I described my symptoms. An odd look crossed her face.

"How old are you?" she asked.

"Forty-one."

"Do you smoke?"

"No."

She checked off boxes.

"Is there a history of heart disease in your family?"

"No."

"There is no way you're having a heart attack," she said, half under her breath, half to me, while looking at the chart she'd just completed on the clipboard.

Her words scared the hell out of me. She was a medical professional.

"You're way too young," she said, shaking her head, but I didn't know whom she was trying to convince.

Soon, another nurse attached electrode monitors to my chest for an EKG and asked, "How old are you?"

"Forty-one."

"Oh, way too young for a heart attack," he decided.

Worried this was all some kind of strange foreshadowing, I wasn't convinced. And I hoped whatever tests they were running would provide some answers and fast.

When the EKG machine spat out a strip of paper, the technician sitting with me quickly retrieved and scrutinized it. He looked up and smiled at me.

"I'll take this to the doctor," he said. "Just relax."

His words were reassuring. Surely if he had seen something unusual, he'd have mentioned it. I breathed out slowly, trying not to worry.

Suddenly, just like a scene out of a movie, a man in a white coat and scrubs grabbed the curtain around me, threw it back, and said, "Ms. Young, we think you're having a heart attack. We're sending you to Med Central as soon as you're stabilized."

Wait—what? My heart wasn't working right?

What if it stopped? I could die.

God, please don't let me die.

This couldn't be really happening.

Nurses surrounded me. One deposited a nitroglycerin tablet under my tongue, while another inserted an IV in my arm, and still another put more monitors on my chest—all while each calmly explained procedures. After I had stabilized, an ambulance would transport me to another hospital about fifteen miles away, a heart-care facility with a reputation for being one of the best in Ohio.

"What's going to happen to me? Will I need open-heart surgery?" I pictured a huge knife cutting open my chest, my heart exposed to the world. It was terrifying. Especially now.

"Well, let's not get ahead of anything," one of the nurses said. "First we have to see what's going on in there."

She explained that upon arrival, I would be prepped for a heart catheterization. A tube fitted with a small camera would be inserted into an artery in my groin and threaded through vessels to look around my heart. I would not be awake for it, and once doctors understood what had happened, they could better assess treatment.

Time seemed to crawl as I waited to stabilize, but inside my mind, thoughts raced. *How had this happened? Had I caused it? Was I going to die all alone on a gurney because I had been too stubborn to let Kenny come with me?*

Kenny. Currently, he wasn't speaking to me.

I had just grabbed my purse and keys when he walked in the door from the garage.

"I'm going to the hospital," I told him as I was leaving. "There's something wrong, and I don't know what it is."

"Should I go with you?" he asked.

"No, I think it's better that you don't," I'd said, but I should have said yes.

I needed to call him.

When he answered, he sounded angry.

"Hull-O?"

What do you want now? he might as well have asked in greeting.

"Hey…uh…I'm…uh…They said I'm having a heart attack."

"Are you kidding?" he asked.

"No. They're stabilizing me, then transferring me to Mansfield for a catheterization."

"Okay..." there was a long pause. "Do you...uh...should I meet you there?"

I was afraid I was going to die. And I knew that no matter what had recently passed between us, Kenny was still important to my life. We had grown up together. He was the father of my children.

"Yes, I think you should."

"Okay, I'll be there as soon as I can," he said and hung up.

I needed to call Mom, too. I had been on the phone with her when I started feeling sick, and no wonder. Ugh.

That phone call. The Bad Husband Litany. Anything she could ever remember—every single bad moment, including those that had slipped my mind. She wouldn't let up, poking the dagger of Bad Husband into me over and over and over, until her reminders turned to pointed comments of contempt. She was worried he would do something to me or my things in retaliation, even though nothing like that had ever happened before. Mom watched too many TV crime dramas.

"You don't think he would ever hurt you, do you, Aimee?" Mom asked.

"Like physically? No, Mom."

"Well, you just never know. That's the way it always happens on my shows," she said.

"Mom, stop."

Suddenly, I wasn't feeling well.

"I worry about you, Aimee," Mom said.

I couldn't respond. A knot had formed between my ribs, and my stomach had risen to the back of my throat like I might vomit. I was warm, so warm. And there was that huge cement block sitting across my chest, so heavy, causing pressure and shortness of breath. *What was this feeling? Fear?* No. *Anxiety?* Maybe.

Something was wrong.

"Mom." I sucked in a breath. "I'm not feeling well."

Was this what it felt like to have a heart attack? No. That couldn't be it. I was too young. But I felt so weird. I started to cry.

"Mom, I'm going to the hospital," I told her, promising to call when I knew what was going on.

She and Dad would leave from Kansas by car that night and drive the twelve hours straight through. Twelve hours. Phew. I hoped they wouldn't be too late, but I didn't say it out loud.

In the ER, once the nitroglycerin started to work, my chest pains stopped and the heaviness lifted. I didn't feel sick anymore, either. EMTs thought I was stable enough to travel, so they loaded me into an ambulance, and we left in the evening darkness for Med Central.

Kenny was waiting there for me, shoulders slumped, head down, hands in pockets. He didn't know what to say, and neither did I.

These were strange circumstances.

After Dr. Pancetta, the cardiologist (an irony I couldn't possibly have made up myself), explained the catheterization procedure, Kenny leaned down to me.

"I love you, Aimee," he said in an almost question.

I was confused. *What should I say?* I did love him, but I wasn't in love with him. I was having a heart attack. I could die, and I might not ever see him again. *Wasn't I obliged to respond?* And yet, only three days ago I had told him I wanted a divorce. In that split second of mind chaos, our relationship and growing up together won out over the end of a marriage. I knew I probably shouldn't say it, but I also knew this was not an ordinary moment.

"I love you, too," I whispered.

The words came out before I could stop them, just like they had when I told him I wanted a divorce, but this time, they didn't hurt. This time, they were the right thing to say.

And then I was wheeled into a very cold operating room where I would be anesthetized for a cardiac catheterization. Doctors would be able to see—from the outside looking in—what was happening inside my heart.

Eight to Nine Days after the Accident

In those first few days following the accident, I'd had four surgeries in the Trauma Center: one to insert chest tubes, remove my spleen, and "pack" me with something to stop the internal bleeding; another to fix my broken foot and ankle; a third to set my broken pelvis and fractured arm; and a fourth to "unpack" my abdomen and place the wound vac.

I couldn't keep track of which doctor was who, and in what medical issue of mine each was interested. Some were young (too young to be doctors, I thought), and some were old. Most were all business, rarely showing emotion. But this morning was different.

A round-faced older doctor whose nametag read Dr. Dowler told me that later I was to be prepped for surgery so they could "close me up" and take out the wound vac.

Another surgery? No. It was too soon. It had been only a couple of days since I had come out of the ICU and off some very scary drugs. I didn't want another surgery.

"Of course, you don't have to be closed up," he explained. "You can let the wound vac stay." His words bounced in a jovial, irritating way.

"I can?"

The wound vac.

According to Dr. Dowler, it was a relatively new—in the past fifteen years—type of therapy. The vacuum, applied through a special sealed dressing, used negative pressure to heal open wounds, and in particular, those of the abdomen. As the vacuum pump drew fluids out of the wound, it also increased blood flow to the injured area.

I had no idea what to do.

"Well, if you return to surgery, you have a twenty percent chance of getting an infection. Not big, but still, something to consider," he said with a smile.

I wasn't finding any of this funny, nor worthy of smiles. I also had no idea what an infection might mean to my recovery, since I was now without a spleen.

"What would *you* do?" I asked him.

He thought about it for barely a moment, turned his head slightly, looked skyward through his glasses, and then said, "Honestly, it's six of one, half-dozen of the other. Either way you go is fine."

He made it sound so simple, like making this decision was no big deal. I almost expected him to say, "If it ain't broke, don't fix it."

I *was* broken, though. And it *did* need to be fixed.

I questioned him about the wound vac and how my abdomen would heal if left alone. He told me that it would take a long time, up to a couple of months, but it eventually would close up on its own from the inside out.

Time. There it was again. An event that had taken less than a second to occur caused doctors to make a split-second decision about my insides that would now take a long time to heal, if indeed it would ever fully heal at all. Oh, the irony.

"Just let the nurse know your decision," Dr. Dowler said.

And then he left.

I was at a complete loss. On one hand, getting rid of the wound vac would mean being attached to one less machine. On the other hand, closing me up meant anesthesia and stitches or staples. Probably stronger drugs. I wasn't even considering the possibility of infection. And I had no idea what healing from the inside out might do to my abdomen.

Mom, who was staying in my apartment and driving almost four hours round trip to the hospital each day, arrived within minutes of the doctor leaving my room. She carried the large iced tea from Wendy's I had requested. But not even the sight of a non-hospital treat perked me up. I cried. I explained what he had told me, and that I wanted my abdomen closed.

"But Mom, I'm scared. I do not want to go through another surgery."

"Aimee, it's your body. It's been through a lot in a very short time. You do what you want to do, and if that means no surgery, then no surgery," she said.

Validation. It was all I needed.

When the nurse came in to prep me, I told her I was keeping the wound vac—no more surgeries. At least not when I had a say in the matter

Mom stood at the foot of my bed, rubbing her hands together. She was not yet seated in her regular spot, the awful orange plastic chair, and now that I had calmed down, I could tell she was upset about something, or at the very least, preoccupied.

"There's a cross where the wreck happened," Mom said suddenly, looking at me, waiting for my reaction. She knew Brian had told me the other driver died in the accident.

At first, no one wanted me to know. I can only guess why not.

Maybe they thought I couldn't handle the stress. Or maybe they worried how the information might affect my recovery

"What's it look like?"

"It's a cross," she said and shrugged. "But it looks like it's made out of Bud Light boxes. I just don't get how people think it's okay to put that there while you are still *here*," she said, acknowledging the hospital trauma room. "I have to drive past that spot twice a day, Aimee. It's hard."

Her tone of voice was changing, her words coming faster.

"I know." I understood why she was upset. Bud Light boxes?

"Well, I've decided something," she said and paused. "I'm writing a letter to the editor of the *Times-Gazette*. It's ridiculous and thoughtless to put that cross there, especially when people who have read about the accident seem to think you're fine."

Fine? They should see me, I thought. A lost front tooth, broken pelvis, fractured sternum, punctured lungs. My abdomen still gaping open. I couldn't move, and I was confined to a bed.

"What do you mean?"

"The paper said you were in critical but stable condition, and when I stopped at the grocery the other day, several people asked about you. Most of their questions assumed you were up and around," she explained. "Look at you! Up and around? You almost died!"

Mom's eyes had filled with tears.

The reality of the situation hit me once again. My family had been through so much these past two weeks. I could be dead, a daughter gone, my children without a mother, a sister lost.

"Mom, don't write a letter. Please."

"Why not?" she asked. She sniffled.

"Because I understand the cross. No one put it there to upset us."

She wasn't looking at me; she was digging through her purse to find a tissue.

"If I had died, people would have done the same for me. I mean, they're only remembering their friend. I get it."

She blew her nose.

"Okay. I won't," she relented. "If you're okay with it."

"I am."

I hated that young man and what he had done, changing my life in a split second, but for some reason, a cross memorializing his death did not bother me. Then again, I was lying in a hospital bed, unable to go there, unable to see it.

I wondered how I would feel when the time came. When I finally did drive past it. Would I be angry? Would I cry? Then I stopped myself.

Quit thinking about driving, Aimee.

You can't even walk.

• • •

I hadn't seen Connor in over a week.

My family had kept him from visiting until I was out of intensive care, breathing on my own, and conscious, which I understood. Otherwise, it might be too upsetting for him. He was only eleven, after all.

Seeing him walk into the room with my mom and Jerrica and Natalie the next day brought such relief—like letting go of a long exhale after holding my breath. All three of my children were here with me, such a comfort after the previous week's chilling experiences.

I wanted to hug and kiss Connor and tell him I loved him, but I worried how I looked. Deep scratches and bruises covered my leg where there was no cast, and a prominent gap filled the space of my missing front tooth. Tubes were coming out of my nose, lungs, arms and stomach, each attaching me to a different machine. I looked as if I—and not the car I'd been driving—had been hit.

Connor walked toward the wall opposite me, keeping his eyes on the floor, avoiding mine. He was probably scared.

"Hi, baby. Come sit. I'm so happy you're here."

I lisped the words through my missing front tooth. I'm sure it magnified how strange it was to see me like this, but he approached the bed half smiling, almost shyly. Even at eleven, he was handsome: an upturned pixie nose, high cheekbones, and chiseled jaw. I hated to think how many girls he would be fighting off one day.

He leaned in for a quick, gentle hug, and I inhaled the faint, still-baby smell of his neck. I rubbed his back, and he stayed there, sitting beside me, while the girls and Mom gathered around the bed.

"Jerrica."

I had not seen Jerrica since I was moved from the ICU two days ago, and even those memories were vague and scattered.

"Hi, Mama," Jerr said, walking over to me.

The oldest of the three, Jerrica looks like me; we have the same smile. Her hug smelled like the soft vanilla perfume she wore every day. I breathed it in deeply, my nose against her blonde hair.

"Hi, Aim," Mom said. "We brought you some things."

It was silly, but secretly I hoped those things included a stuffed Clifford dog. I was eager for a sign that God had really been watching over me. When that stuffed red dog never appeared, I tried not to be disappointed.

Jerr stepped aside and Mom set a plastic grocery bag down on the small dresser beside me so I could see what was inside.

Treasure! My shampoo, beat-up wide-tooth black comb, round brush, and blow dryer stuffed the bag. Tucked down inside, in its own Ziploc bag, was my tattered and faded blue baby blanket. Yes, I was forty-one, but I still slept with that blankie under my pillow every single night. The knotty, thin cotton against my fingertips meant comfort, safety.

I couldn't help myself: I opened the bag, reached in to feel the fabric, and pulled it up to my nose. I inhaled the familiar scent of security and smiled.

Everyone laughed.

"We also brought you these," Natalie said.

She walked over and handed my purse and cell phone to me, then leaned in for a hug. Again, I breathed in the comforting scent of my child.

More treasure! My purse contained a small makeup bag of just the essentials, maybe enough to even make me feel human again, and my cell phone was my lifeline to the outside world. Both had been in the car with me.

"Dad took us to where your car was to get those," Jerr said. "Your phone was clear up underneath the dash where the gas pedal is."

"Wow—I'm glad you found it. Thank you."

"Guess what else we found when we went to your car?" she asked.

I had no idea. Jerr moved forward and put one gold hoop earring in the palm of my hand, part of the pair I had splurged on just a few weeks ago.

"Ooooooh…you didn't find the other?"

"No," she said. "We looked, but we couldn't find it."

I turned the smooth metal between my fingertips, scrutinizing it. When I noticed dried blood on the inside surface of the hoop, I set it down. I didn't say anything, and I didn't show them. I wondered where the earring's match was. I wondered if it was lying on the ground, in the grass, near the Bud Light cross.

Suddenly, I wanted to know what I looked like.

My appearance was important to me—it always had been. "You're such a princess," Mom had once told me, and she was right. Nothing was more important to my personal grooming ritual than my hair, eyelashes, and nails (hands *and* toes)—in that order—and I spent about as much on them per year as I did on my health insurance.

Right now, I was definitely *not* princess material. It had been over a week since the accident, and my hair still had not been washed. For all I knew, neither had my face. I felt icky, itchy, and greasy. I wanted to be clean again.

When my nurse came into the room next, she noticed my comb and makeup bag lying on the tray.

"Oh, how nice—do you need a mirror?" she asked.

She pushed in a levered button on the side of the bedside tray table, and the top tray slid back, revealing another tray and a small mirror. I leaned forward slowly and peered into the reflective glass, squinting at my appearance so I could see every detail.

I looked atrocious—like a scary, wild witch from a fairy tale. Yes, I was still me, but a drastically rougher, uglier version.

My full, chin-length bob hairstyle was flat, stuck to my head, and greasy with dirt. My eyebrows were wild, hairs marking the places that had not been tweezed in so many days. Dark, half-circle shadows sat below tired, sunken-in eyes, where a trace of eyeliner and mascara were still evident. My nose had a small scratch and my bottom lip, a slight cut. I opened my cracked, dry lips to see what I already knew I would find—the missing front tooth.

I held my mouth open and looked at the hole from all angles. Finally, I tried out a smile, grinning into the mirror.

Tears filled my eyes. I'd had a beautiful smile. I got compliments all the time. Yes, it had always been crooked—two front teeth at a teeny angle and a bottom row squeezed together—but it was still beautiful. The "best smile" in the class of '87.

Now it was gone.

I looked up at the kids and Mom and shrugged my shoulders in defeat. I looked like a frightful, deranged madwoman. The perfect appearance I strived for every day had vanished, and I was embarrassed.

"Mom. You look fine," Jerr scolded. "You were in a horrible accident—what do you expect?"

"I know, Jerr, but it's my front tooth."

"And it can be replaced," Jerr said. "You can't."

She was right. I was stuck in a bed, hair smashed against a pillow, remnants of makeup around my eyes, and with a missing front tooth. But my visitors didn't care how I looked, and I had nothing but time.

Time: The only thing that could heal a broken heart, the only thing that could heal a broken body. Also the only thing that could heal a broken appearance.

I had plenty of it.

July 2004

Once upon a time, I met Cinderella on the red carpet.

The Cinderella.

And *the* red carpet. (At least as close as a middle-aged teacher from rural Ohio would ever get to it.)

I was one of thirty-nine teacher-winners attending the prestigious DisneyHAND national teaching awards ceremony in Disneyland, "the happiest place on Earth," and two of my dreams were coming true. Since college, I had hoped that one day I could be so loved and lucky as a teacher to win something like this, but even more than that, I was meeting my fairy-tale heroine, a permanent fixture of my life since early childhood.

I was only four years old, fresh out of the bath and cozy in pajamas, when my little brother and I were loaded into the family station wagon, duped into thinking we were going for an evening drive to see one of Dad's summertime paint jobs. Probably a barn. The summer sun was setting as our young groans—surely this would be the most boring drive of our lives—turned to shrieks of excitement when we pulled into the Springmill Drive-In. Walt Disney's *Cinderella* was playing on the big screen!

Mom and Dad rolled down the car windows, hooked up the speakers, and we jumped into the front seat. Enchantment ensued, and I haven't been the same since.

Cinderella. Her name was beautiful, her story fanciful, and I wanted to be just like her.

Now here I was next to her, as a teacher celebrating my DisneyHAND award, cameras flashing, a string quartet playing, and Minnie and Goofy frolicking nearby. We stood side by side, Cinderella and I, two perfect princesses with arms around each other's waists, both dressed to kill. She wore vintage, one-of-a-kind ball attire, and I sparkled in a glamorous, beaded, black gown.

We smiled and posed for photographers, and someone snapped our photo just in time to capture the unmistakable, childlike look on my face that said it all: *Ohmygod, it's Cinderella!*

I was in awe of her, unable to speak.

And then, as if it had turned midnight, she was gone, and I hadn't gotten to talk to her. I wanted to tell her she was my favorite princess and that I felt like her that night. That this small-town high school teacher and mom of three had been transformed into a lovely sight for all in the Land to see. And that I was attending this grand celebration with family, too: my parents, my brother and his wife, and my could-be-charming husband.

Wait a second. Where was Prince Charming? And why wasn't he with Cinderella? Uh oh. Something wasn't right.

But I was distracted, and she moved on.

Then I saw her, selfishly searching out others for flirting and photo ops on the red carpet, and I knew I had been fooled. *That* Cinderella, no longer partnered with her fairy-tale mate and only interested in getting attention, was a fake. *That* Cinderella turned out to be a disappointment.

Years later, I would realize why the lingering mark of that symbolic moment stood out to me: that moment of foreshadowing took root in my own story. A seed was planted, a transformation began, and I grew into an image of the Cinderella I'd met in person: a perfectly fake disappointment.

"You know, you had the perfect heart attack," the intensive care nurse said while checking my vitals.

I was in recovery, and Dr. Pancetta had just been in to tell me what they found during the catheterization.

The heart attack had been caused by an arterial dissection. Part of my artery's wall had broken away, causing blood to flow between the layers and forcing them apart. This initiated the attack, or myocardial infarction, as it's called in the medical world. By the time Dr. Pancetta did the catheterization, the arterial tear had "miraculously" repaired itself. There was no blockage or plaque buildup, and no stent was needed.

I was confused. Even curious.

"A perfect heart attack? What do you mean?" I asked. The thought was laughable. Everyone knows heart attacks are bad.

"I mean, if you had to have a heart attack, you did it the right way," she said and smiled. "No blockage, only a little damage to the heart, and you're still alive!"

Only a little damage—ha! If she only knew. But she was right. It was perfect. My broken heart had fixed itself. I wondered how long the cure would hold.

Only hours before, I had been on a gurney in the hospital's ER, alone and afraid I was going to die. I still couldn't believe it. *I* had a heart attack?

Dr. Pancetta and Dr. Fams, the other cardiologist assigned to my case, both asked me the same questions, though at different times and on different rounds.

Do you smoke, Aimee? Do you have any history of heart disease in your family? Are you a drug user?

No, no, and no.

As a generally healthy forty-one-year-old woman with no risk factors who'd suffered a heart attack, I was an anomaly.

Hmmm. This is strange.

When each grasped his clipboard in one hand and flipped pages in bafflement with the other, I felt like I should tell the truth.

The words, hanging there in that hospital room's stale air—"I told my husband I wanted a divorce three days ago"—sounded heavy and odd. They were so new. Unwelcome even.

But full of explanation for a heart attack.

Ahhhhh, I see. Makes sense.

"What questions do you have?" Dr. Fams asked. His tall, kind presence filled the room, which seemed to shrink around us.

"What am I going to do now?" I wanted to ask him. *"Where am I going to go when I leave here?"* But he didn't have the answers to those questions.

"Could it happen again?" I asked.

I didn't think surviving a heart attack was as common as dying from one, and I had made it through alive. I didn't want the same thing to happen once I left the observation of doctors and nurses.

He sat down in the room's chair then and leaned forward.

"The heart attack you had will most likely *not* repeat itself."

He explained that the spontaneous arterial dissection could mean weakened arteries and the potential for another "cardio event," so they were admitting me for a few days of rest and observation to be cautious.

"We're pretty sure that your arterial dissection and heart attack were caused by high blood pressure and stress," Dr. Fams said. "We've prescribed medicine for the blood pressure, but," he paused, "once you're home, you *have* to find new ways to deal with stress."

Home. Yikes. Where was that now?

Jerrica had already asked me if I was coming home, and her question, full of assumption, surprised me.

"No, Jerr, I'm not. I can't."

I knew that wasn't the answer she wanted to hear. Her life—Natalie's life, Connor's life—had just been turned upside down. I knew she expected what every kid would: Mom would come home and heal, Dad would take care of her, and she would forget about the divorce, the cause of the stress.

"Well I don't know why not," she said. "Obviously, you need rest. You need to come home."

Everything was so black and white to teenagers.

A flash of guilt brought the faintest fluttering of anxiety across my chest. *Should* I go home? No, that would be crazy. "Home" was part of what caused this. Of course I didn't want to be away from my children—all I had known for seventeen years was being *with* them, caring *for* them—but I also couldn't imagine what going home might mean right now.

Any mom knows that the *last* place to go expecting rest is home.

Plus, a piece of my heart had been damaged there.

I didn't respond to Jerr, and that was the end of it. She didn't try to talk me into coming home again.

"I understand that you're in a tricky situation with your husband, but your health has to be the most important thing right now," Dr. Fams went on. "What do you do for a living, Aimee?"

"I'm a teacher. Twelfth-grade English."

"More stress?" he asked, a smile peeking out from under his dark mustache.

"No, not really. This is my eighteenth year, so I'm used to it by now. How long will I be off work?"

"Six weeks. And in a few, I want you to start our cardio rehab program. I'll get you some information," he said and left.

The hospital's twelve-week cardio rehabilitation program was made up of two components: classes on managing diet and stress, and an exercise regimen, all for the sake of learning how to live a heart-healthy life. Cardio fitness trainers would design a workout just for me, and my heart would be monitored while I did it, three times a week, at their facility and on their exercise equipment.

Six weeks off school to rest, a personally prescribed exercise routine, and coaches to encourage me along the way. Just the way to start my new life.

Perfect.

II

"After a while you could get used to anything."
~Albert Camus, *The Stranger*

Nine Days after the Accident

"Hi, Aimee?" an unfamiliar female voice asked after knocking on the door frame to announce her presence.

"Yes?"

A fresh-faced, slender woman in light blue scrubs pulled back the curtain. She couldn't have been more than twenty-five years old.

"I'm Danielle from Physical Therapy," she said. "I'm going to get you up and moving again."

She had brown hair, big eyes, and a perky energy that reminded me of a favorite student teacher of mine. Instantly, I felt at ease.

It didn't last long.

"Already? Like *right now* up and moving?"

Mom was in the awful orange chair by the window reading. I saw her look up at this and raise her eyebrows, but she didn't say anything.

It had been only nine days since the accident. It was too soon.

"Yep! Gotta get those muscles working," the therapist announced.

Danielle started by putting me through a few basic arm and leg exercises to gauge my mobility range and strength. There wasn't much of either.

"Do you think you can sit on the edge of the bed?" she asked.

I hadn't actually moved on my own since before the accident, because nurses had been helping me. I was scared.

"I haven't tried yet. How do I do it?"

I was surprised to hear my own words. I had to actually ask how to move my own body, one I had lived in for forty-one years. And now I was a stranger. First, it had been in my own home, as an intruder grabbing all my belongings to move into a hotel. Now it was my own body, as a foreigner getting my bearings to adapt to this new land. Both places I used to belong. Until expulsion.

"You can only put weight on your right arm and leg, so use them for leverage and balance," she instructed. "Try to push yourself off the bedrail there, and move the rest of your body around until your legs are hanging over the side. Think you can do that?"

I could tell she was not going to help, that this was a test. She stood away from the bed to watch. I didn't want to do this yet, but I knew that eventually I'd have to try. And maybe if I did, she'd leave sooner.

"I'll try."

I used the bed controls to lift the mattress to as close to a sitting position as I could get, then I put my right hand on the bed rail. I grasped it tightly and pushed hard, scooting my body down the mattress while turning and lifting it at the same time.

I grunted, slowly pivoting left, but I barely moved. I was dead weight.

The cast on my leg felt like it weighed fifty pounds, but I managed to inch my legs over a little at a time, until I ended up half on and half off the edge of the bed, almost on my side. I laid there for a moment, catching my breath and wondering why I agreed to this.

"I can't do it. I can't sit up."

"Yes, you can, Aimee," Danielle said. "You're almost there. Try."

I knew she was right. And I couldn't keep lying in this position, twisted and uncomfortable.

I put my right arm behind me and pushed against the mattress to boost myself. Everything inside me tightened, and somehow, I found the strength to pick myself up and move my legs a little more. Finally, I was sitting, hunched over and breathless, on the left side of the bed. I felt like I might collapse from utter exhaustion. The last several minutes had sucked right out of me what little energy I had. I couldn't believe how hard it was to move. I had been a lump in a bed with over a dozen fractures and punctures for well over a week now, and it was a minor miracle that I could actually sort of sit. How would I ever walk again?

"Aimee, that was awesome—you did great," Danielle said. "Now you need to stand up."

"Are you kidding?"

"No, I'm not—but only long enough to get from the bed into that chair," she said.

Sure, yeah. I'll just stand, Danielle.

Man, was she pissing me off. Had she not just witnessed my struggle to the edge of the bed? If and when I finally did stand up, I thought I might punch her.

I sat on the edge of the bed feeling woozy and like I might fall backward. Danielle set a walker in front of me that was different from any I'd seen before. This one had a single handle—made for someone who could only use one hand—and it looked tricky.

She bent down to move all of my tubes and wires aside.

"Now I want you to grab the handle of the walker with your right hand and lean on it while you lift yourself off the bed. Don't use your other arm, and don't use your left leg. Just this side." She gestured with her hand from my right shoulder down to my right thigh.

"But how am I going to do it? I don't think I can."

I didn't feel strong enough. It was one thing to use my good arm to scoot myself down the bed and into a seated position, but quite another to lift the dead weight of my useless, fractured body while balancing on my good arm and good leg.

"You have to use your core as support, Aimee, your abdominal muscles," she explained.

Yeah, well, my "core" had only recently been cut open, moved around, and left to close up on its own. Wasn't reading my chart a part of her job?

But I kept quiet, sitting there staring at the walker. I couldn't wait for her to leave.

"Come on," she said. "You can do it, Aimee."

I hated her.

Lean on one hand and lift up from your core.

I grabbed the handle of the walker with my right arm and pushed down, hoping it would give me a start. Nothing happened. My rear end was like a powerful magnet, begging for that bed, holding me down. I struggled to pick myself up and realized I had no strength in any part of me—the fractured parts, the non-fractured parts, nothing. I grunted, pushed down again, and tried from deep within to lift myself. Again, nothing.

Time stalled.

I couldn't move my own body.

In just nine days, my body had transformed from a normal standing, running, walking, dancing, climbing stairs, and moving body to one that felt like it was paralyzed.

I had been reduced to inert mass.

I tried rocking to gain momentum. I must have looked like a huge, blue hospital-gowned blob, swaying and grunting and shaking, my left arm hanging uselessly at my side, the heavy cast cementing me to the bed. The rocking lifted me enough to quickly fall sideways, gravity having other plans. Danielle grabbed one side of me and Mom grabbed the other, while I groaned the words, "What now?"

Their strength held and then turned me slightly, setting me down in a chair.

"Do you think you can sit there for a bit?" Danielle asked.

"Maybe."

I was panting, winded.

She did it—she succeeded.

Danielle went to work with other patients, and Mom went to find something for lunch. All I could think about was doing the same thing all over again to get back in bed. I was already so tired.

"How are you doing, Aimee?" Danielle asked when she returned.

"I'm ready to get back into bed."

"So soon?" she asked. "I'd really like to see you sit there a bit longer."

I had been sitting, hunched over, in this uncomfortable, plastic, wing-backed chair for several minutes—an eternity. The huge sponge-covered wound of my abdomen ached from slouching, and I was tired from moving. I wanted to be back in bed.

"I can't. I'm hurting."

She gave in, telling me she was happy with my progress, and helped me return to my only comfort. This time, relying on her strength, I let her do the work.

"I'll be back tomorrow, and we'll do it all over again."

Danielle smiled and waved as she breezed out of the room and on to her next victim.

I felt sick.

Tomorrow was far too soon.

I hated my body and what it had become. It wasn't mine—my body had been new and improved after the heart attack. I had worked out three times a week for twelve weeks with trainers in cardio rehab, getting healthy, toned up, and strong again. And for the last month since rehab had been over, if I didn't walk during my hour-long lunch break from my summer writing workshop, I danced with my girls in preparation for drill team camp.

But the last four months of getting in shape didn't matter. Not to this body.

I could barely move. I couldn't pick myself up to stand on my own two feet. And it hurt, everything hurt.

I didn't see how waiting until tomorrow would make any difference.

• • •

Getting up and out of bed the day before had taken a toll, and somehow, I had pulled a muscle in my back. The pain was excruciating. Sharp, knifelike pains reminiscent of childbirth stabbed my lower back in waves, incremental but constant.

I lay there crying, wishing for something, anything, to take it away. None of my injuries had been this painful, and I still had two more hours to wait for my scheduled pain meds.

I buzzed the nurse anyway.

I was twisted left, positioned on my side, head tucked into my shoulder, when the nurse arrived. She saw I was crying, something I hadn't done yet because of pain. She told me she could bring something to get me past the "break-through" pain until my scheduled meds time, and it worked. My muscles relaxed enough to let me rest.

When doctors made their rounds later, one of them mentioned that in a few days I should start working with the physical therapist to get out of bed.

In a few *days*? I couldn't believe it.

What about all the anguish of yesterday? Not only was I suffering from traumatic injuries inside and out, but now I also had muscle strain from moving around and getting up. I knew in some part of me that it had been too soon, but Danielle had been adamant, and I'd felt I couldn't say no.

When I told the doctors about my visit from physical therapy, they were surprised. They told me to wait a day or so for further movement, and they would let the physical therapist know. I knew that eventually I'd have to try to get up and move again, but for now, I could rest.

Danielle arrived a little while later, which was unexpected. When I told her what the doctors said, she was obviously taken aback. Lines were getting crossed somewhere, but that wasn't my problem.

I was not getting out of bed. Doctors had told me I could wait. End of discussion.

Her stoic, cold expression said she had other plans, however. Her job description: get people who don't believe they can move to move. So that's just what she would do. End of discussion.

But not me. Not today. I just couldn't.

And more importantly, I wouldn't. It was my body, my decision.

"Can we please just try again tomorrow? I can't move my back at all. I think I pulled something yesterday."

She didn't know me—she didn't know that I'd give anything to be able to get up and use the bathroom or walk the hall. All she knew was that her patient was not cooperating. And when she continued to persevere, show no sympathy, and explain why I should get up, I cried. *Again.*

Seeing my tears, she managed a smile, said yes we could try tomorrow instead, and left. Just like that.

Victory.

Oh, thank God, I thought as I exhaled deeply. Without realizing it, I had been holding my breath.

I pushed the tears from under my eyes with the fingers of my good, right hand and relaxed into the cradle of the hospital bed. I knew Danielle would write "refused therapy" on my chart today, but this new body needed rest from the strenuous work of the day before.

Besides, there was always tomorrow.

And I wasn't going anywhere.

• • •

The days and nights in the Trauma Clinic faded in and out of one another, one right after the other, broken up only by visits from hospital personnel or my family. Hospital-bed existence became routine.

My body was an oxymoron, new to me but broken, and I didn't understand its limitations yet. Within the first few days awake, I watched my roommate hobble back and forth to the bathroom, wishing so badly that I could do the same. I wanted to sit on a toilet or wash my hands. I wanted to splash water on my face and brush my teeth.

It would be easy, I thought. I could favor my left side and move with my right, balancing my weight on the side with strength. Then I could just hobble to the bathroom using anything around me for support. *I could do it, couldn't I?*

The response from my nurses was a resounding no. Using the bathroom was off limits—that was made clear—but they *would* take my catheter out, as long as I used a bedpan. I agreed, having no idea going to the bathroom would be one of many things I would never take for granted again.

The refrains of recovery: Get your rest. Your body heals more quickly when you're sleeping. Aimee, you need quiet.

The reality of recovery: constant interruptions.

My blood was always drawn in the wee hours of the morning, interrupting what little sleep I got, and soon I became an expert at knowing which phlebotomist needed more practice and which did not. Because of the chest tubes, my lungs were X-rayed for fluid by the same handsome technician who visited before breakfast every day, always smelling like he was on his way to a date. My daily meds were also administered before breakfast, but those for pain came when necessary throughout the day, most times alternating with my vitals being taken.

Aides washed me in the mornings, changing the bed sheets around me, almost always right before the doctors' rounds. Teams of doctors visited each day, making me feel like a science experiment or, as my brother had put it, a "miracle." The wound vac pump, as well as the fluid from my chest tubes, had to be drained every few hours, the dressings changed every couple of days. The scrapes, incision sites, broken bones, and my IV were also checked during each nurse's shift, just in case the one before had forgotten.

I couldn't turn on either side because chest tubes stuck straight out of the skin under my arms. If I spent too long on either hip, the dull pain of a broken pelvis turned persistent and sharp. I couldn't move my left arm, heavy and achy with metal, or my left leg—the cast had it cemented to the bed. My broken ribs and sternum hurt the worst, like serrated knives poking or jabbing my lungs if I breathed too deeply or coughed. And my abdomen was a gaping wound, covered only by a sponge; the area around it was bruised, swollen, and tender.

Discomfort was non-stop—even the slightest jarring reverberated through my entire body. So I stayed at a forty-five-degree angle, and I learned how to fall asleep on my back. Sleep happened only at the most random times—typically after pain medication, and not surprisingly, just as a meal was arriving—but rarely at typical hours and never when I tried. Most nights, I turned off the TV around eleven and shut my eyes, waiting for sleep. Quiet, sterile gray darkness would settle over the room like translucent gauze, while nurses' muffled voices went to and fro outside the door, but I just lay there awake and annoyed.

Danielle came every day. Sometimes, twice a day. I dreaded seeing her walk into my room, even though I knew she would stay for only a little while. Sometimes she put me through exercises and sometimes she didn't, but she always had me get up and into that chair. I managed to sit for longer and longer periods, usually eating my lunch or watching TV there, until my abdomen or pelvis couldn't take the discomfort any longer. I got stronger and stronger, improving slowly in my ability to control my strange new body, but those bits of time exhausted me.

Some days, getting back into my bed made me feel guilty, but it was where I lived. In fact, my whole world was within an arm's reach. The tray to my left held my makeup bag and nourishment— snacks, leftovers I was saving, and ice water, and the bedside table to my right was stacked with my laptop and a pile of reading material—novels and gossip magazines. Confined to a bed for who-knows-how-long, I would actually have the time to read, an English teacher's dream.

But I just wasn't interested. And it just wasn't enough to keep my mind busy. I couldn't focus enough to read anything of real length.

I would open a magazine or book and read a few sentences only to stop and think, *Who cares?* Facebook updates on my laptop were about all I could manage. When I watched TV, I stayed away from the news, usually getting lost in the cooking of Food Network or the competition of *So You Think You Can Dance.* I just didn't care, couldn't care, about people I didn't know, whether real or fictional, and their trivial tales. I didn't have the energy to empathize with them when I had worse, more significant things affecting my life.

I hated that someone had done this to me. I was also lonely there in that bed. I had just started to gain control of my life in a new apartment near my children. My relationship with them, strained from the divorce, had been improving.

Then wham! Out of nowhere, the control was gone, and I was undone, dismantled to my very bones.

I was so angry. *What had happened to my life? Was God punishing me? How had I survived when the other driver hadn't, and everyone told me I shouldn't have?* So much guilt.

Night after night, these questions plagued me, overwhelmed me, and the longer I stayed in that hospital bed, the more I felt cocooned and safe from their answers. Actually, even if lonely, I felt cocooned and safe, period. People here took care of me, fed me, tended to me, and made me comfortable. I didn't know if I would ever want to leave the safety of this protective new home.

Outside was a scary, uncertain world where your life could change in a split second.

You could have a heart attack all alone without anyone around to help.

Or a car could fly out of the darkness, smashing you to pieces.

A Week after the Heart Attack

I needed to get my things. Whatever I could fit into Mom and Dad's SUV, anyway.

I had lived in that house a long time—twelve years—long enough to believe I would never leave the safety and protection of the home where my own family lived. I knew the front door would be unlocked, but I was still sneaking in on what felt like a covert, secret mission. And with two accomplices: my parents.

They had insisted on bringing me, just as they had insisted that I was not returning there to live. Worried about stressing out my already weakened heart, Mom and Dad had reserved a suite at the Hampton Inn for me until my new apartment was available.

No one was home now: The kids were in school, Kenny was at work, and we were intruders.

I wanted our visit to go unnoticed, but I knew that anything I took would disturb its physical environment and whatever normalcy was still intact for the children. Mom's "stuff" was there, and for them, that's where it belonged. If my "stuff" never left, I would eventually come home.

But it didn't feel like home any longer.

We left the beige curtains in the front picture window and at the back sliding door—the curtains Mom and Dad had bought us as a housewarming gift—drawn, and we didn't turn on any lights. There was no need in the bright afternoon light, but it added to the furtive feel of this "robbery."

I ignored Bear, who followed at my feet as I zipped through the house, thinking she was too old, too deaf, and too blind to know I was here, but she did. We had rescued the poofy little schipperke ten years ago, and though she was most attached to Jerrica, she thought of me as her second master. She kept up with me all through the house, but I didn't acknowledge her. I didn't reach down and pet her once. I couldn't.

I fled from room to room, collecting things that were mine and handing them off to whomever was closer, Mom or Dad. What I needed for everyday living. Anything decorative I wanted. I moved from the walk-in closet to the bathroom cabinets to the bedroom dresser, passing items off to my mother or father to load into their silver Honda Pilot. All my clothes. Makeup. The blow dryer and flat iron. The framed 8-by-10 of Ricky Martin. My jewelry box. My Mickey Mouse trophy from DisneyHAND. Books. I focused on guarding against emotion, aware and afraid that if feelings bubbled up, I could collapse in tears or worse: chest pains.

Don't risk the stress. Keep your heart safe. Flee the guilt. The quicker, the better. If you forget something, the kids can bring it later.

I moved to the living room's front closet and retrieved my jackets and coats. I turned and looked at my living room furniture. The barn-siding tables Kenny had made for me for Christmas one year. The new couch and loveseat we had purchased in the fall. I started to feel dizzy. I wondered who would get what. I would fight about it with him later. I looked up at the family portrait on the wall over the TV, taken eight years before. Things seemed easier then, before tearing apart my family. I consciously looked away and grabbed framed photos, wall art, and candles. But not the family photo. I couldn't.

Should I check the basement? No, there was nothing of mine in Jerrica's room, and I didn't need high school memorabilia or old photo albums right now.

What about the other kids' rooms? Should I peek in? Natalie's across from Connor's. Newly painted chalkboard walls with Natalie's friends' graffiti greeted my glance, surrounding a teenaged mess. I turned, opened Connor's door, and made sure I had left nothing in the army camo-covered bottom bunk. The pillows smelled like him.

Don't think about it don't think about it don't think about it . . .

I had to get out before I broke down, and I hadn't even been away an entire week yet. Coming here was harder than I thought it would be.

A last look around, a final stop in the kitchen. No dishes or crock pot or wine rack. No time—just go.

The rectangular oak island in the center of the kitchen caught my eye then. Inside, below the green marble top, important papers and files: birth certificates, immunization records, social security cards of our three babies, tax records, the certificate of marriage. Something flashed through my mind about needing past years' tax filings for divorce paperwork, and I reached in to pull the folders out from among the discarded bills and bank statements, evidence of our recent bankruptcy. Maybe these important things should stay under the roof where the children lived. I set them down, wavering. Then I snatched them up to take. I was the mom, after all. The responsible person of the family.

Family. *What family?* There was no family now. I had destroyed it, and I wondered if my children would ever forgive me. The children. Three people I love more than life itself.

What would Jerrica, Natalie, and Connor think when they got

*home from school? How would they feel actually seeing what I had
taken, knowing I was really gone? Would they feel like I had aban-
doned them? And what was their father saying without me around?
Could they really understand that I had to leave?*

Maybe I was being selfish, sacrificing the last eighteen years to
find some sort of happiness I hadn't felt in a long time. All I knew
was that anger and boredom had come to control me, the woman
who had lost herself. The old, happier me had been lingering for
some time, quietly tugging at my shirt sleeve because she knew not
to interrupt.

But she did anyway.

I climbed into the back seat of Dad's Honda, the last one out of
the house. Both Mom and Dad turned around to look at me.

"Did you get everything you needed, Aim?" Dad asked.

"Are you feeling okay?" Mom questioned.

"Yes and yes," I said, turning my face from them to look out the
window. I didn't want them to see my eyes filling with tears or have
them tell me I was doing the right thing. I didn't want to share this
horrible, terrifying moment with them any more than I already
had. And I certainly didn't want to talk.

Dad backed the Pilot out of the driveway onto the street and
pulled away from the curb, and I stared straight ahead. I just had to
keep looking forward.

Two Weeks after the Accident

"Ms. Young?"

It was yet another doctor, but this time, in the middle of the afternoon. Visits by doctors at any time of the other than morning rounds were not good. It meant they couldn't wait until the next day to let you know whatever it was they found.

"Yes?"

"I've just read your morning X-rays, and you have a chip fracture in your right wrist," she said.

My wrist had been hurting, but a nurse's quick assessment had turned up nothing. When I complained to doctors on morning rounds about it, they explained that immediately after the accident, I was assessed for major injuries only. It was possible for minor injuries to go unnoticed, particularly when the patient was not coherent enough to express pain.

So to make sure nothing had been missed, they sent me off to be X-rayed, Jerrica and Natalie by my side.

That was a couple of hours ago.

"*Another* broken bone?"

I couldn't believe it.

"No, not a broken bone, a *fracture*, a crack, and in this case, a chip," she explained.

That didn't make it sound any better. Brian and I already had counted eighteen fractures in my body, and now there was one more.

Nineteen fractures. Almost ten times the number of fractured bones an average person experiences in her lifetime.

Before the accident, I'd had only one broken bone, of which I'd been vocally proud. My prideful words reminded me of being a child bragging about never having been stung by a bee. No sooner had I boasted than I stepped on a live nest, the stings too numerous to count.

"But I've been doing physical therapy every day, and I've been putting weight on it. What will I do now?" I could hear myself whining.

My right arm was the only means of freedom I had. I used it to eat, to move myself around in bed, to grab what I needed, to help with the bed pan, even to blow dry my hair (the couple times it had been washed, that is). I didn't want the one thing allowing mobility to be taken away. I almost wished I'd never complained in the first place.

"You really shouldn't use it at all," the doctor said. "It has to heal."

Oh, no. I had to fight this. The worst that could happen was that she would ignore my pleas, and I would have another cast. (And bad hair.)

"But I've been using it for a week, and it hasn't really hurt. It's the only way I can really move my body around right now!"

"Hmmmm," she said, eyeing my wrist again. "There's no swelling, and it has been two weeks since the accident. If I put a splint on it that you can remove, do you promise to at least keep it on during physical therapy?"

"Of course!"

I was almost giddy with excitement—over retaining the freedom to put pressure on another fractured bone.

My world was small right now, my movement limited. I didn't need another obstacle when I already had so many to overcome.

It was a small victory, but it was still a win. And I had impressed myself with my own assertiveness. If there was one thing I was learning in here, it was that if I didn't speak up for myself, no one would. No one else knew how it felt to be lying where I was.

"Since you're here, can you take a look at the cast on my leg? It's so heavy, I can barely move it."

She lifted my leg to see how it was fitted.

"I don't see why it can't be changed, but let me ask," she said and smiled.

I liked her. She listened to me.

Later when the cast was cut off, I saw what I hadn't imagined was beneath: an extremely hairy, bruised and scraped leg from the knee down, and a very swollen, black-and-blue-all-over foot.

A lengthy, jagged scar marked the middle of my foot where the bones had come through. There was also a wire sticking out of my foot which fascinated me, because I had not felt it under the thick, dense cast.

My leg was placed in an open-front, molded plastic brace that enclosed the back of my knee down to the tips of my toes, curving to cup the sole of my foot. Cushioned and blue in color, the new cast was held in place with nothing more than an Ace Bandage wrapped around the length of it. The nurse assured me that even though I had a broken ankle, this lighter cast would still provide necessary stability.

"Besides, you really aren't up and moving around that much," he said.

Which I knew, of course.

But what a difference the new cast made: from a back-straining cement block to a cottony-light cloud. I could finally lift my leg without feeling like I was going to tear a thigh muscle in the process.

• • •

I heard her arrive, moaning so loudly I wanted earplugs. It seemed as if all hell had broken loose in my previously quiet, sterile environment.

Nurses pulled the curtain around my bed for rest and privacy, but that thin, flimsy, plaid room-divider was a joke. I lay in my bed at the back of the room, trying to mind my own business, but I overheard most everything through that pseudo-curtain of privacy.

When the nurse asked her what had happened, the patient's words came out swollen and muddled. Something was wrong with her mouth or jaw. I tuned into her language as if she had a foreign accent and found out her face had been cut so severely by the breaking glass of the car's windows that it was affecting her speech. She cried, moaning between words, begging for pain medication the nurse said she couldn't have yet.

She claimed her boyfriend had tried to kill her: they were riding in a car she was driving when he became furious with her, told her he should just kill her, and then yanked the steering wheel. The car rolled several times, and neither of them was wearing a seatbelt.

I felt my own jaw drop in horror. The nurse's silence said that she was as incredulous as I. I continued to listen intently, while the nurse asked the appropriate questions.

The woman's boyfriend, uninjured in the wreck, left her and the car at the scene of the accident. He walked away from her, leaving her lying in the mud by the car's tire.

Her story startled me and shook my sense of safety.

The injured woman's parents and toddler son came into the room, and I heard them request that the boyfriend not be allowed to visit. The hospital, however, could only keep all visitors from coming in or none, because it was too hard to stop just one person.

I was unnerved, stunned that the possibility existed for him to come into "our" room after trying to kill her.

The injured woman assured her parents that he wouldn't show up anyway, and soon they said their goodbyes and left.

We were all alone.

"Hey! You over there! Call the nurse in here!" she bellowed.

I froze.

We were each assigned our own nurse; there wasn't one assigned to the room. I had been here long enough to know that much.

"There's a big button to push on the side of your bed," I answered meekly.

"I realize that," she snarled. "It won't work!"

I called my nurse. I could tell she wasn't happy about needing to fetch my roommate's nurse, but she did it. I was embarrassed and apologetic. After almost two weeks here, I knew how hard the trauma floor nurses worked taking care of so many patients.

My roommate moaned and wailed waiting for her nurse to arrive, after which she begged and cried for more pain meds. She must have gotten them, because she quieted some.

Her nurse left and we were alone again.

Then, her bedside phone rang. I heard her muffled, low "Hello?" Then the sounds of her crying. It was him. It was her boyfriend.

"You tried to kill me!" she screamed through swollen lips.

It got quiet as she listened to what he had to say.

Then she said she loved him and that she wanted him here.

Was she crazy?

I was stuck in a bed, unable to walk, barely able to move, and fresh off my own trauma, and she was inviting someone who wanted her dead to come to "our" room. *What if he came to see her, they got into a fight, and I was the witness who needed silenced?*

My newly healed heart fluttered in fear. I wanted out of that room.

I texted my mother—I didn't call, because I didn't want my roommate to hear. Mom had been my advocate thus far, a constantly present force in the hospital every day. I was sure that once I explained the situation, she would take care of it.

I waited for her response text, which seemed to take forever. I knew she had gone out to eat with my uncle, but I also knew she would keep her phone nearby just for me. Her text back was nonchalant, not worried, an "Oh, wow" response. I wished I could call her, but I didn't dare take the chance.

Wait a minute. I was the only person who knew how I felt. My safety and peace of mind were being threatened after living through the most horrific trauma of my life. I was a grown woman who had also survived a heart attack. And I was entitled to be assured I would not die in a hospital room by the hands of some stranger's maniacal boyfriend.

I had to take control, because this time I could. This time I could get away from another young man's poor decision-making. I needed to talk to my nurse.

When she appeared, I motioned her closer there behind the curtain. She understood, moved to my side, and leaned down.

"I don't want anyone to hear," I whispered before explaining my fears.

"I don't blame you," she whispered back. "I'll see what I can do."

She pulled the curtain back to take my vitals, long enough for me to see my roommate being wheeled out of the room for X-rays: she was young, her hair a ratted mess, and her face looked as if Dr. Frankenstein himself had sewn it back together.

Within minutes, the nursing supervisor came in to let me know they were moving me to another room.

I had asserted myself when it mattered, spoken up for myself without someone else's help, and it had worked.

Phew.

• • •

"We're calling you Humpty Dumpty, you know."

His name was Dr. Peterson, and he was the orthopedic surgeon who had performed three surgeries on me in the days just after the accident. He wasn't surrounded by a team—a pleasant surprise—and I could tell from his handshake that he was kind.

"You are?"

"Yes," he replied. "We had to put you back together."

He said it without humor or irony, but then he smiled.

Humpty Dumpty. The riddle turned nursery rhyme. Just my luck. All this time I had wanted to be a perfect princess, and instead I was being compared to an irreparable egg that had fallen from a wall.

I guess it fit. I had shattered, too, my body's framework in pieces. But all the king's horses and all the king's men *were* able to put me back together again. At least physically. And here he was, finally, representing the troops.

I had been wondering when I would meet him—Mom had spoken so highly of him and his care these past couple of weeks—and I could see why. In addition to his gentle demeanor, he looked like Harrison Ford. Hmmmm. Indiana Jones was not quite *my* version of Prince Charming, but he was still a modern-day hero. And he had saved my life.

Dr. Peterson spent the next several minutes gently explaining the repairs he had made to the breaks of my body, where they were located, and what different pieces of metal were holding them in place.

As he came around the bed to leave, he stood at the edge and looked down at me.

"I know this may be hard to believe, Aimee, but a year from now, I will have you ninety percent back to normal."

My eyes filled with tears. I nodded in understanding.

"Thank you."

And then he left.

A whole year to recover. Three hundred and sixty-five days. A lot could happen in a year. My life had fallen apart in just five months. And now, it would take a year to heal. Even then, he promised only that I would be ninety percent back to normal.

Just a week ago, another doctor had told me they *thought* I would make it, and now I knew I would never be one hundred percent normal again. But it didn't matter.

I didn't know what normal was anymore.

• • •

Mom would be helping me transition from patient to independence, staying with me as my live-in nurse when I returned home from the hospital, for as long as it might take. As long as I needed.

"Until you can stand on your own and tell me to get out," she told me.

Just like that, it was decided. Just like moving into a hotel room after my heart attack was decided.

But I didn't argue. I didn't even consider another option. *Were there other options?*

Mom and Dad had packed their car and left in the late-night hours after finding out about the accident. Dad had to fly back to Kansas City for his job, but because Mom was an independent computer analyst consultant, she could work from anywhere.

So she moved her office into my Loudonville apartment, the third place I'd moved to since leaving home. Mom already had been staying there, driving daily to Cleveland to visit me, check my progress, and keep watch over my care.

This morning, she was perched in the ugly orange chair at the foot of my bed with her laptop open and on. She wanted to show me the photographs of my car after the accident. Dad had somehow tracked down the towing company in the days following and taken pictures.

I wasn't sure why she wanted me to see them now—so soon—but I would take a look. Maybe she thought it would help me to better understand what had happened to my body.

I wasn't prepared for what I saw.

My 2008 Saturn Aura, the color of "ocean mist," crumpled up, mangled, and folded in where his red Mini Cooper had made impact just below the driver's-side mirror at the wheel well. The windshield, lifting at the corners, shattered around its perimeter. The driver's seat twisted back, angled the direction it had been jammed, steering-wheel airbag deployed and spattered with blood. More blood spatters all over the seats, dark stains against the gray cloth interior.

I was shocked. Disgusted. And I didn't know what to say.

How *had* I survived?

And what the hell was that kid thinking? I wanted answers—I didn't care if he was dead.

Hot, silent tears squeezed from the corners of my eyes. I was sickened looking at the photos of my broken car.

Mom had to have known how I would react. She had to have known they would upset me. Still, I didn't say anything. She was driving every day to be with me. She was taking care of my place. She was paying my bills. And she was probably dealing with her own form of grief. She had probably needed to share the photos with someone; I just wished it hadn't been me. Not yet.

When doctors arrived for rounds, I put the pictures out of my head. I didn't want to think about them any longer. Three or four doctors surrounded me in my bed, alternating questions.

How are you feeling today? How is your breathing? Have you been eating?

Aside from their different nationalities, they were all young and male, they all wore white coats, and each had a clipboard and pen in his hands. They formed a single medical entity, none distinguishable from the others.

After I answered their queries, I had questions of my own for them.

"When will I be able to return to work?"

"What do you do, Aimee?" one said.

"I'm a high school English teacher."

"Well, it all depends on your continued recovery," he said. "Fractured bones take at least six weeks, so you're looking at a minimum of two months."

It was the middle of August now.

"So I could possibly be back in school by October?"

The doctors exchanged glances, raising eyebrows. I could tell they thought October was a bit too soon to return to work.

I didn't like the fact that I would be missing the beginning of the school year. Setting the tone for the semester was always an important part of teaching, and it was hard to take time away from the classroom when you cared about students' education. Last year, I had missed six weeks in the spring because of the heart attack, too.

Just then, the doctor nearest Mom noticed the photos on her laptop. Maybe what was happening was exactly what she had intended. Maybe she had even gotten his attention somehow to look at them. They began talking while she showed him the pictures, though I was in the middle of my own conversation.

"October? It's always possible," one of the doctors said.

"Okay, next question: When can I go home?"

"Well, that's a little trickier," another doctor said. "You're going to need physical and occupational therapy, which means a nursing facility as a bridge between here and home. You live on your own, correct?"

"Yes."

"Do your children stay with you?" he asked.

Sore subject, I wanted to say.

"Sometimes. But my mom"—I nodded in her direction—"is going to be staying with me until I'm better."

They turned to her. "Is that right, ma'am?"

Mom and the doctor looked up from the laptop when we got quiet waiting for her response.

"Yes," Mom said. "I told her that I'd stay until the day she could literally stand and kick me out of the door."

The doctors laughed.

"You are very lucky, Aimee," the doctor who had been looking at the pictures said to me. "For the extent of damage that was done to your car, you could be in a *lot* worse shape."

I didn't know what to say. He meant dead. I could be dead.

Fucking Zach Ryder. This was all his fault. And he *was* dead.

"Is there any type of therapy here that Aimee could get so she doesn't have to move someplace else before going home?" Mom asked.

"Yes, actually. We have a rehab floor here she can go to, but," the doctor paused, looking at me, "you would have to agree to a few hours of physical and occupational therapy every day."

"That's fine by me."

"Okay, then. We'll start the process to get you transferred, but you need to continue getting better and stronger so that we can get you up and moving," the doctor said.

Phew. No nursing home. I gave them a tired smile, and they said their goodbyes.

I wondered how soon before I could start the rehabilitation for home. I wondered how my new body would respond to movement and exercise that was different from Danielle's work. I wondered what it would be like to have my mother living with me, taking care of me at age forty-one, while at the same time I wondered who would take care of my seniors at school, since I couldn't.

And then I wondered if I would ever be able to forgive a high school kid I didn't know who might have changed my life forever.

Eight years after I started teaching English at Loudonville High School, also my alma mater, my Building One classroom moved from Room 114 down the hall, around the corner, and into Room 110.

It was an administrative, geographical alignment of subject areas, evidently, and one that excited me to no end.

Once upon a time, Room 110 had been the classroom of my favorite math teacher, Mr. Matthews, who had taught me all four years of high school—long enough for me to develop a huge teenage crush. And he knew it, too. I blushed when he called on me, I blushed when he walked into the cafeteria and my friends yelled, "Hey, Aimee," and he blushed all the time, victim of a ruddy complexion that I found so—*sigh*—attractive.

A few years after I'd inhabited the room as an English teacher, Mr. Matthews stopped in my doorway on a random visit to the high school one afternoon. He wanted to say hi, check out his old room, and I, instantly sixteen again, wanted to faint. I stood frozen beside my desk, a safe twenty feet away, grinning in surprise.

"Mr. Matthews!" I shouted. "This is your room! And I teach in it now!"

How obvious. How embarrassing.

He smiled politely, said it was good to see me, and left.

I wondered what he thought of his room's newest décor.

Just like way-back-when, two large windows still framed the

acres of farmland behind the building, but the oversized drafting desks and clumsy equation "cheat sheet" poster boards of Mr. Matthews' were gone. The two, built-in graphing chalkboards were now covered with a map of Great Britain and a poster of me with Mickey Mouse, and between them, a map of the world was pinned to the room's only bulletin board. The far corner of the room housed a map of Nazi-Occupied Europe and various photos from my visits to Holocaust sites in Poland.

Technicolor movie stills from the *Wizard of Oz* covered the doors of my book cabinet, and a brilliant collection of Hallmark cards my sister authored sat among the framed photos on top of my filing cabinet. Books and vocabulary words that "every high school graduate should know" bordered the eclectic assortment, but the *piece de resistance* was my Ricky Martin photo collection.

And it all added up to one thing: my classroom.

A typical day in high school English usually meant a discussion analyzing some piece of brilliant classic literature—my escape. Like the time a few years ago when my AP Lit and Composition class had just finished Albert Camus' *The Stranger*, a book no one liked to read but everybody liked to talk about.

I had written the most simplistic explanation for existentialism I could come up with on the chalkboard just minutes before class started.

To exist means to suffer. And to live through that suffering, we find meaning in our lives.

"So, why did Meursault shoot and kill the Arab?" I asked.

One student said Camus' book was a joke. Another thought he was being a hypocrite, while yet another student agreed, "Yeah, the book makes no sense."

"Because Meursault is just Holden Caulfield all grown up," someone else said, trying to be funny.

Everyone laughed. I loved when students made literary jokes.

"Meursault doesn't even cry at his own mother's funeral," another student added.

"Well, that's a good point," I said. "Who doesn't cry at his own mother's funeral?"

"*The Stranger* is about some dude shooting some other random dude on a beach after a lot of wine," another student said. "That's it."

Everything is so black and white to teenagers.

But maybe, I told them, just maybe, there was more going on. Maybe Camus was trying to tell us something. Or express his beliefs. I explained that Camus believed that life had no rational meaning, and because humans struggled with this, they constantly sought meaning. He also believed that people longed for immortality, even knowing that existence comes to an end. Life then, Camus thought, was an unending struggle toward nothing but death.

Blank stares. A "huh?" or two or three escaped a few mouths.

And then my teacher thing took over, my brain scanning its files to find an example—something to share—to help them understand.

"What about school shootings?"

Since I started teaching in 1992, fifteen school shootings in almost as many states had left more than seventy people dead and numerous injured. The killers ranged in age from twelve to thirty-two, and the educational settings varied from a one-room Amish schoolhouse to university campuses. All violent, and most of them random.

"Aren't we all trying to make sense out of something senseless? And isn't that human nature?"

No matter how many of the killers in school shootings had histories of mental illness, and no matter how many times the patterns of school shootings were analyzed, none of it would ever make sense. We would never be able to say, "Oh, that's why he did it."

"Yeah, but those shootings are real life," someone responded. "What we're talking about is a *book*."

"But literature echoes our lives," I said, "and what we are touched by daily. And sometimes, literature even underlines truths that we don't want to confront."

Truths about living and loving and suffering and dying.

"Sometimes, it's no use to figure out a character like Meursault, because it can't be done," I said. "Because sometimes that's what the writer intends. Because sometimes that is the meaning we're looking for."

Sometimes qualities exist that we can't quite name or define, showing us new ways to look at the world while revealing fresh perspectives, even about ourselves.

And isn't that the beauty of the writing and the literature itself?

Faces around the room looked thoughtful.

"I like the book a little better now that we've discussed it some," someone said.

A few others echoed with "Yeah" and "Me, too."

Common understanding and appreciation: all I was going for. Analyzing and thinking critically about literature and its lessons wasn't as complicated when you could see life around you—maybe even your own—reflected through it.

To exist means to suffer. And to live through that suffering, we find meaning in our lives.

How ironic those words then, how true those words now.

Spinal Cord Injury Rehabilitation Clinic |
Three Weeks after the Accident

Moving to the rehab clinic brought a whole new existence for me: one of increasing autonomy.

But it came with a price.

I had to agree to over an hour of physical, occupational, and recreational therapy five days a week, and thirty minutes more for one day a week.

Six days of therapy every week, learning how to use my muscles again, seemed unimaginable to me, especially when I was still confined to a bed.

But I was willing to try. After all, it meant I was one step closer to going home.

Therapy also meant it was time for real clothes. A hospital gown just wouldn't do for the types of movement and exertion I was expected to tackle now.

When a nurse's aide came in to help me get dressed for my first visit to the therapy center, I surprised her by putting on my tank top with one arm and mostly by myself. I needed help with the bottoms, though. My abdomen was still attached to the wound vac and so swollen that she had to get a pair of loose scrubs. She removed the ace bandage and plastic cast from my leg and foot, and I inched the pants over them, being careful not to bump anything. When it was time, I leaned back on the bed and lifted my rear, while she pulled the scrubs up around my waist. Then she put my cast back in place and slipped a sock over my good foot.

It was time to transfer to the wheelchair.

My new wheelchair, measured to fit only me: shiny and black with chrome handles and footrests. My new best friend. A means of freedom and getting out of bed. It meant using an actual toilet by myself instead of calling a nurse to help with a bedpan. It meant leaving the confinement of a hospital room. A wheelchair meant going home.

I couldn't wait to try it out.

The aide pushed it beside my bed, locked the wheels' brakes, and asked if I was ready.

Of course I was, thanks to Danielle. Danielle had been the task-master I needed.

I was already sitting on the edge of the bed, so using my good arm and the bed's railing, I lifted myself up, putting weight on my right foot, while she held me around my waist. I grabbed the arm of the chair, she pivoted me, and gravity plunked me down on the seat. It took just a few more minutes to place my legs on the footrests and hang the portable wound vac from the back.

"Am I going to wheel myself there?"

"No, today I'm going to take you," she said. "You'll learn how to move around in it once you get to the gym with the physical therapists."

She wheeled me out of the room, down the hall, and through a doorway into an adjoining facility, the physical therapy gym.

People were everywhere. Different kinds of people: people in scrubs, people in wheelchairs, people on crutches, people with walkers, people in white coats, people in street clothes. Men and women, elderly and middle-aged. They were sitting around tables, standing by other people, or lying on square makeshift beds. Some played cards or worked on games, some lifted limbs in exercises, some guided others through those exercises, and some sat looking back at me.

This was a busy place.

It was also strangely quiet. Only the sounds of low voices, piped-in music, and the occasional movement of someone nearby could be heard.

I was fascinated by the scene, my eyes darting here and there as she pushed me slowly through the large rooms. So many people needed rehabilitation. So many broken people.

Like me.

And then I saw him, the guy Mom had been telling me about.

A big man, broad-shouldered and burly. He was a Hell's Angel who had lost his leg in a motorcycle accident. My parents had shared a crowded waiting room with his friends while we were both patients in the ICU. He had long gray hair thinning on top and an even longer beard. He was struggling to a sitting position on a square sort of bed, his right leg missing from just above the knee.

He was angry, too. The scowl on his face and the coarse tone of his voice as he yelled at the therapist standing beside him made that apparent. His new body was frustrating him.

When the aide pushed me past, I averted my eyes. Even though we had something in common, I decided not to strike up a conversation. He was scary, and I felt guilty. My body was new, too, but all of my limbs were intact. I would eventually gain my freedom back, but he, well, he would always be limited in his.

And then it hit me once again: I was lucky. Lucky to have gotten out of that crushed car alive. Lucky to have survived my injuries.

Those times, the luck was about survival.

But the lucky I was feeling now was different. I was alive, yes, but there are all sorts of ways to be alive and unlucky.

I could be the one missing a leg or an arm. Even paralyzed. I could have been left with brain damage, or unable to breathe on my own, or without the function of my kidneys. I could have had my face cut up beyond recognition.

Huh. How about that. I was lucky. Again, maybe even a miracle.

For the past two weeks, I had been feeling so sorry for myself, when I really should have been feeling thankful. The Universe had protected us that night—it was evident in my memories, it was evident in those photographs, and it was evident by my injuries.

But it's hard to be thankful when you're angry.

• • •

I spent three hours a day in physical and occupational therapy, and I hated it.

I complained about it.

I even tried getting out of it.

But I also knew that it was preparation for leaving. I had nothing better to do anyway.

In those first days, physical therapists had to pick up my shaking body, too weak to move on its own, and set me on the square, wooden bed's red exercise mat. There, I did the minimal work required. I couldn't wait to go back to my room and get into my bed.

Even so, the physical therapists were a breath of fresh air, a welcome break from the grumpy nurses of the Spinal Injury Rehab floor. Patients were always coming and going, and most times, the therapists were dealing with the frustrations of ten of us at once. Still, they remained positive and welcoming, special kinds of cheerleaders. The scopes of their jobs were fascinating—they worked with so many people. People in wheelchairs, people without limbs, people behind walkers.

People who were damaged—some beyond repair—people like me.

But my challenges were minimal next to some, a thought I tried to keep in perspective. My new body gained strength, and in just over a week, I had progressed from arm- and leg-lifting exercises to making my own wheelchair transfers and hopping without the use of my one-handed walker.

Occupational therapy, however, tested me in different ways. Here, simple tasks to work my fine motor skills were more difficult than I anticipated: playing games, putting puzzles together, moving a little plastic car around a peg board, balancing on my good foot for minutes at a time. All to improve my eye-hand coordination and reflexes. Soon, I was also practicing gross motor skills like getting from the wheelchair onto a bath seat in a tub or in and out of a vehicle.

As therapy got easier, I realized that going home would soon be a reality, and that scared the hell out of me.

Here I had the care and protection of nurses, physical therapists, and a hospital room.

Home was an old, roomy apartment I'd moved into only two months ago and where my mother would live with me playing nurse. How would I *really* take a bath or get out of a car or maneuver my wheelchair? Practicing to do it, which was really pretending, wasn't the same as actually doing it. My body was so fragile and scarred.

And yet I'd witnessed its resiliency. Physical therapy had taken everything out of me, but I kept pushing myself to move.

The desire to go home paired with the fear of leaving safety.

Just months before it had been the desire to leave safety paired with the fear of leaving my children and making a mistake.

My, how quickly things change.

Suite Number 304 at the Hampton Inn: my first "new" home. The place to start my also "new" life.

Sounds like a commercial, doesn't it? *"Come stay with us and restart your life! Enjoy your new freedom in a room at the Hampton Inn!"*

One large room all to myself in a two-star-rated, standard hotel. A place for transitory, impermanent, or temporary dwelling. How ironic, this new freedom of mine.

I was a mere traveler, a tourist in my own life. I didn't belong anywhere anymore.

But maybe it was best: a gentle, stress-free dipping of toes into the foreign pool of independence. There was no new living space to furnish (yet), there was no need for cooking (yet), and there was nothing to clean (yet). I had two queen-sized beds, a chaise lounge and couch, a TV and desk, and even a kitchenette. The suite's cost included a hot breakfast buffet, and I could venture to any one of numerous fast-food establishments or even Walmart. I also had housekeepers and front-desk clerks who catered to my every whim.

I imagined them sharing my story in the linen storage or behind the front desk. I was the lady who'd just had a heart attack—"It's true! And she's only forty-one!"—after splitting from her husband. I was a sad story.

And so I lived there for almost a month, waiting on my apartment to be available.

My parents insisted on it.

But I was alone and living without my children, half an hour away from them.

The center of me, the balance of my universe, was missing. I had been an active, present mother for seventeen years with three children who spent every day of their lives with me. I kissed them goodnight each and every night.

But they had stayed at their home. And their father wasn't enforcing any kind of a visitation schedule.

This strange new life wasn't natural, and it certainly wasn't the way I had imagined it.

A part of me was relieved to be away from the responsibilities of wife and mother, the craziness of daily decisions, chores, and stress, but guilt crept in. I wasn't taking care of my children, and I should have been. I didn't want their father filling the role that I had for almost eighteen years, particularly when he usually stayed on the sidelines. Why was I the one who had to leave?

And yet, maybe this was what I needed after a heart attack: the disquieting quiet of a lonely hotel room. I just didn't know how I was supposed to heal without my children.

Jerrica, Natalie, and Connor.

I missed them desperately. Natalie's chronic morning sniffles and TV snuggle time with Connor every night. The echoing "What's for dinner?" from three different mouths, the groans or sighs following the reply. The never-ending pile of kids' dirty laundry.

I couldn't wait for my apartment to be ready. Once out of the hotel, I was sure the kids would be around more, and together, we could start a routine for them staying with me on a regular basis. Together, we would make a new home.

But that didn't happen.

• • •

After three weeks of living in a hotel, I moved into my second "new" home: the bottom quarter of a huge, old house on the main street of Ashland, a half hour from Loudonville and worse, still a half hour from my children.

"Mom, are you allowed to have pets?" Connor asked me when he visited for the first time.

I had left behind our schipperke, Bear, and three cats.

"No, I'm afraid I can't," I said, frowning.

"But Mom, don't you miss them? Don't you miss Bear and Alex and Oliver and Mo? You used to see them every day. Maybe you should come see them. Or, hey, maybe they can come with us to your place sometime!"

He was eleven and didn't quite understand.

"Yes, baby, of course I miss them," I said. "And someday, when I have my own house where we can have pets, we will. I promise."

I wanted to cry.

But not now. Not in front of Connor.

Yes, I missed my pets, but I missed living under the same roof as my children even more. And I hated Kenny. He refused to make an alternating schedule work, letting the kids stay wherever they wanted, and of course I knew where that would be—in their own beds with their pets. It was punishment—the worst kind—and he knew it.

Night after night, I sat in my brand-new chaise in my brand new "home" staring at the TV, wishing I was somewhere else. Somewhere my children were. I kept a tissue in one hand to wipe away the tears, a glass of chardonnay in the other to sip away the pain. I cried every night. I drank every night.

Not only was I living without my kids, but I had been shunned by old friends and acquaintances who had sided with Kenny, especially obvious at softball games for the girls. I was stared at, talked about, and pointedly ignored. I left many games—and sometimes even the small-town grocery store—alone and crying, guilt overwhelming me once again.

I shouldn't have been surprised, really. In fact, a friend of mine had even warned me.

"So what's going on? Something's been bothering you," Carol said. She leaned in and lowered her head, looking me in the eyes.

We were at a writing retreat, and she could tell I needed someone to talk to.

"I think I want a divorce."

I hadn't said those words out loud yet. I was still thinking, planning, gathering advice and information. Carol was the first person I had told—I knew she would be honest with me.

"You know, Aimee, some people are going to think you very selfish for this," she said in her soft, gentle voice.

I blinked the warning away. I blew it off.

"Oh, I'm sure they will."

My reply then was flip, but now I knew Carol had been right: People did think I was selfish. Maybe even stupid.

Still, I didn't understand. How could they judge me when they had no idea about my marriage, my relationship, my life? And how was it any of their business?

From the outside looking in, you'd never know.

I was no longer a wife, barely a mom, and I was caught between two worlds: the one I had just left and the one I wanted so badly. Who was I, and what had I done?

• • •

I caused my own heart attack.

Not like when you smoke three packs of Winstons a day, or you can't breathe after climbing a set of stairs, or you eat bacon and red meat and fried foods.

Not like that.

Doctors, who are much more knowledgeable than I on the subject, have said my heart attack—an "anomaly"—was caused by high blood pressure due to stress, and I believe them, I do, but I wondered if more was going on. So, I researched.

I came across Broken Heart Syndrome and wondered if I'd found something that fit.

Heart disease is the number one killer of both men and women, but Broken Heart Syndrome, also called Takotsubo ("octopus trap") Cardiomyopathy, is a real thing. Harvard Health Publications say that up to five percent of women evaluated for a heart attack have this disorder, which can be brought on by strong emotions, such as grief or anxiety. And according to PBS NewsHour, ninety percent of broken-heart patients are women, who are ten times more likely to suffer from Broken Heart Syndrome than men. Google also says there are more than 200,000 cases per year.

The American Heart Association says that Broken Heart Syndrome, or stress-induced cardiomyopathy, is usually misdiagnosed as a heart attack because the symptoms are similar, though there's no evidence of blocked arteries. The occurrence of a stressful event causes adrenaline and other stress hormones to surge, which also causes shortness of breath, chest pain, sweating, nausea, and vomiting.

Just like what happened to me.

Cardiologists believed I had an arterial dissection that had "miraculously" repaired itself by the time they performed the heart catheterization. They'd said there had been only a "little damage." I also had no blockage.

All broken-heart patients studied recovered within a couple of weeks, unlike a person who has a massive heart attack and never gets back to normal. I was discharged from the hospital after just three days.

But the tipping point was finding out that all broken-heart patients had experienced some profound emotional sadness, significant emotional shock, or physical stress. That was me, too.

Yep. Self-diagnosis: Broken Heart Syndrome.

I didn't, and still don't, take the vows of marriage lightly. As a girl dreaming of my future husband, I was adamant about divorce: it would *never* happen to me. I believed in love. I believed it was the only ingredient a relationship needed to succeed.

But maturity proved my girlish idealism wrong—it didn't hold up.

I wanted that happily ever after; I really did. But I didn't feel it anymore. And I couldn't keep my promises any longer. I hurt someone I cared about. He threw his wedding ring at the wall. The cruel metallic clink still haunted me.

And then I hurt Jerrica, Natalie, and Connor, the people most vital to my life—my heart.

I had broken my own heart.

I needed to be near my children. They were far more important than my privacy and relief from a nosy, gossipy town, anyway. They were my normal.

So, before the school year ended, I moved back to Loudonville and into my third "new" home: the downstairs half of an old, drafty

Victorian house with a beautiful wrap-around front porch and dark, original woodwork. I knew the kids wouldn't live with me, but they were within reach again, and that was all that mattered.

Soon, the dirty laundry, 50,000 pairs of running shoes, teen magazines, and hair ties piled up around my new place, and I started to smile more. My kids were a happy invasion and close enough to be around every day, a necessity for my sanity.

Time really can heal a broken heart, because I felt more like myself than I had in four months. Life started to settle and my heart started to mend. The muscle had been gaining strength through cardio rehabilitation, and its hollow chambers were filling with the substance necessary to maintain a regular rhythm again.

Maybe it would beat stronger than ever.

And it did.

Until the night of July 27, 2010, when a young man's car crashed into mine, leaving its permanent mark on my life.

"Your belly button! You still have it! How wonderful!" the nurse changing my wound vac dressing exclaimed.

I had come to dread the dressing changes. Maybe she was making small talk to take my mind off it.

"Sometimes they can't save it, but yours is still here!" she continued.

My belly button. The first permanent scar of my—of everyone's—body. I hadn't even thought about it.

As she pushed and squeezed the skin surrounding the gaping wound of my abdomen, I winced, wishing this were already over.

"When you're finished with the dressing change, could you please check under my arm? Something hurts."

Each movement of my arm felt like it was rubbing against swollen, raw skin where the chest tube in my right breast had been removed.

"Of course," my nurse said.

First, she removed the old dressing. The vac's swath of black sponge was covered in a clear plastic film that stretched rib to rib and down the length of my abdomen, like a window into my body. I wondered what they saw from the outside looking in, all these doctors and nurses, through this window behind a sponge.

The plastic came up with no trouble, but the foam sponge was another story. Because it fit just inside the wound, removing it was always uncomfortable. Depending on which nurse was doing the change, sometimes it was downright painful. Today's nurse used the saline spray to loosen the sponge, making it much easier to peel up, thankfully. Phew.

Once the old dressing was removed, the rest was easy. The skin around the wound was sprayed with a protectant so the drape's adhesive wouldn't tear the tender flesh, and then the wound itself was sprayed and cleaned with gauze. A new sponge was cut to fit, placed in the wound, covered with plastic drape, and the vacuum attached to the center.

The nurse turned on the wound vac to check for leaks, but this time, there were none.

"Okay, let's see what you've got going on here," the nurse said, moving the wound-change extras aside. "Can you lift your arm for me?"

She peeled back the bandage covering the hole under my arm.

"Oh my," she said. She pressed the area around the wound and asked, "Does it hurt when I do that?"

I flinched.

"Ouch! Yes!"

"You've got an infection," she said. "I'll have to get a sample to send to the lab."

She grabbed a piece of gauze to soak up the pus and continued to press. She swabbed the area just inside the hole for a sample of the bacteria, then cleaned and dressed the spot that had recently held a tube to drain my lung. Once the pressure was released, the pain under my arm was almost entirely gone. Phew.

An infection couldn't mean much, right? Just some Neosporin on the wound and a little more time. At least, that's what I thought.

Wrong.

• • •

I had MRSA. *Methicillin-resistant Staphylococcus aureus.* A staph infection. Just what I needed. Staph infections were notoriously bad.

The doctor who brought the bad news told me this type of infection was common—at least among people in hospitals or other health-care facilities—but because of that, it had become resistant to commonly used antibiotics.

Since my spleen, the body's source for fighting infection, had just been removed, and antibiotics might not work, I was at extra risk. I had to be put in isolation, because I was a source for transmission to other patients, particularly those with weakened immune systems.

Quarantined.

Doctors and nurses would have to wear special protection and use caution in my care so they wouldn't spread the bacteria to other patients. My children and family could still visit—yay!—but they would have to be careful, as well.

I had been on the Spinal Rehab floor for only three days, and I was being moved away from other patients. Now I didn't even fit in among people like me, who had undergone their own traumas and needed rehabilitation. The prospect of having my own room— freedom for the first time in three weeks—didn't even appeal to me, and tears rolled down my cheeks.

Why me, God? Why me? Why did that kid have to hit me? Why was I going through all this after suffering a heart attack? Wasn't that enough? When would I start to feel better? When would all this end?

I sobbed. I sniffled. I wallowed.

"You stop that, ya hear?"

The quiet words surprised me. They had come from my room-mate, a middle-aged woman who didn't talk much. Until now.

"You stop that cryin'," she repeated, scolding me.

The thin plaid curtain that might have separated us had been pulled back, exposing us to each other. I looked over my left shoulder to make eye contact with her.

She was sitting the same way she had been for the past few days that we'd shared the room: in a chair that looked like a sling, made of cloth and metal, both arms and legs extended, parallel to the floor. She could not move or walk.

"You goin' be fine, but I—well, I—who knows," she continued slowly.

I didn't know her name, but I knew she was married and a mom. Two small children and their father had visited the other evening, but she couldn't even hold the youngest on her lap. Both kids, probably under the age of five, had been content to watch TV and color while their parents talked.

She looked so tired now, slumped against the back of the chair, and much older than she probably was. Whatever was wrong with her had taken its toll on her sad face, but she tried to smile.

"May I ask what happened to you?" I asked.

So far, I had been careful to give her privacy. We had barely spoken to each other.

"They don' know. Test after test after test, and they just don' know." She paused, grunted. She was in pain.

"But you, you goin' be fine. You *will* heal. You *will* be well again," she nodded.

And then she leaned her head back against a pillow and shut her eyes, while her words bounced around the inside my head.

I dabbed at my tears with a tissue, digesting her gentle reprimand. A woman who had no idea what was wrong with her own body, who seemed to have conceded to an unknown disease, had just given me a pep talk. A woman who might never be able to embrace her children.

I felt guilty. And embarrassment for being so self-involved.

But I also hoped she was right. That I *would* be okay and that I *would* heal. From what I understood, MRSA was pretty serious, and I still wasn't sure how it might affect me.

Later, as a nurse helped me into my wheelchair and pushed me to the door, I turned to look at my roommate one last time. She was quiet there in her sling.

"Goodbye. And thank you."

"Bye," she said, attempting a smile. "Good luck to you."

Luck, I thought as I was wheeled from the room. Not this time. What I needed to be well was medicine, doctors, time—so much time—and hard work.

Within the week, the intravenous antibiotics necessary to fight the staph were switched to oral capsules—the infection was healing—and the physical therapists gave their blessing for my discharge. The woman had been right after all. I was ready. My broken body was mending.

Follow-up appointments and home nurses were scheduled, the portable wound vac arrived, and Mom packed up my room. I was heading home, exactly one month—to the day—after the accident.

This Cleveland hospital had advertised itself as the "proud sponsor of the comeback," and now that was me.

III

"Things don't go away. They become you."
~Darin Strauss, *Half a Life*

In the fuzzy, floating seconds after impact that warm July night, between the recognition of splintered bones and the reality of crushed metal, I remembered wondering how long this accident would inconvenience me, how long until I could get home.

I never imagined it would be thirty-two days.

I still needed medical attention on a regular basis but not enough to take up a bed in a rehabilitation center. I could get around my apartment in the Victorian with my wheelchair or walker, and I had Mom for help. She had inhabited my spare bedroom shortly after the accident and now she was to be my live-in nurse, caring for me just as she had when I was a little girl. I was grateful to have her here, but at the same time, at age forty-one, I resented having a babysitter.

Whatever medical needs of mine Mom couldn't handle, home health-care nurses would. They were scheduled to visit several times a week to change my wound vac dressing, check my injuries, and make sure I was healing.

My first appointment was set for the morning after I returned home.

As soon as she arrived, Sharon, dark-haired and petite, held out her hand and introduced herself as an RN from an area home-nursing company.

"I'm just going to review your hospital notes here, and then we'll get started," Sharon said as she pulled a file from her bag and smiled. She had a kind face and a gentle manner.

Sharon had read from her files, turning many pages, when I heard her say, "Oh." She had encountered a surprise about me—probably all of the fractured bones, or maybe my punctured lungs, the ventilator. Maybe she hadn't been expecting so many injuries.

"I see here that you were resuscitated?" she asked.

Resuscitated. The word echoed in my head.

Had I heard her correctly?

"I'm sorry?"

Sharon looked up from her paperwork and smiled again.

"You were resuscitated," she said quietly. "Did you know that?"

I was stunned. No one told me.

Resuscitated?

I swallowed and shook my head.

"Hey, Mom? Can you come in here?"

Mom appeared almost immediately. She must have heard something in the tone of my voice that worried her.

"Sharon said it's in my records that I was resuscitated."

Sharon nodded, as Mom turned to her with wide eyes.

"Oh, wow," Mom said. "We didn't know that."

Sharon looked back down at the paperwork again.

"It says right here that you were in hemorrhagic shock due to blood loss and had to be resuscitated," she explained.

My body had lost so much blood because of internal bleeding that it had gone into shock. The blood-thinning medication I took because of my heart attack probably had made things worse. I remembered Jorden yelling from behind me in the car when the voice at my window wanted to know who I was: *That's Aimee Young! She's had a heart attack before!*

And thank God she did. The EMTs and the doctors where I was

first taken might have acted more quickly in assessing me and calling for Life Flight because of it. In fact, Jorden probably saved my life that night. With that much internal trauma, every second would have counted, and Jorden's smart warning might have saved me from going into shock mid-air. Sharon said I had been resuscitated in Cleveland shortly after the helicopter's arrival.

Resuscitated.

Revived.

Dead or almost dead.

The other driver had died that night, and now I knew more precisely how close I'd come to dying, too.

The rest of Sharon's visit was what I expected: she checked my vitals and injuries, asked about my medication use, and changed my wound vac dressing. But what she had told me about being resuscitated rattled me.

I needed to think about it.

I stopped living. Doctors brought me back.

I thought of the voice I heard in the car that night—strange, quiet, and firm. Almost otherworldly. *Stop moving or you will die.*

It couldn't have been an EMT, because they were outside the car. This voice was inside the car, right beside me. In my ear.

A warning. The voice knew how serious my injuries were before doctors, even EMTs, did.

Stop moving or you will die.

And I had. Almost.

"Can you believe that?" Mom asked after Sharon left. "After everything you've gone through, now we find out you were..."

Resuscitated, I thought, as her voice trailed off. Sharon's announcement hung in the heavy summer humidity of my living room.

Tears filled my eyes, and my chin started to quiver.

"Do you remember it?" Mom asked. Then as an afterthought, "Hey, did you see a white light or anything?"

Her comment took me by surprise, and I giggled, even as I cried. I knew she was trying to make light of the situation because she didn't want me upset. And we've all heard about those near-death, crossing-over-the-brink, white-light/bright-light experiences.

I shook my head.

"Mom, no."

"I'm just asking," she said. "That's what they say happens, you know."

I replayed the loop of memories I had from that night in my mind just to be sure. No lights, no visions, nothing. Just that voice in the car, cautionary and guiding.

"I don't remember anything after they put me in the helicopter."

"Wow," she said again.

I was horrified once more by the magnitude of that life-changing split second. One young life was gone before he'd even really lived.

His injuries were fatal. He couldn't be saved.

But I could.

• • •

Before I knew it, I had settled into a comfortable daily routine that revolved around TV shows and meals, unless Mom was chauffeuring me to any number of scheduled medical follow-ups. The first, while still in my wheelchair, was with my family dentist to see if he could fix my broken smile. I was embarrassed and self-conscious without my front tooth.

After looking at the damage done inside my mouth, Dr. Steve recommended dental implants for both teeth—the missing one in the front and the broken one in the back—and an oral surgeon to start the process. It would be time-consuming, taking anywhere from six months to a year or more, but he assured me the results would be worth it.

"Quite frankly," he told me, "you should get permanent implants. You did not do this to yourself, and you have the right to have your teeth back the way they were."

I fought back tears. Someone understood. *He* understood.

Dr. Steve had summed up in one sentence how I felt about my entire life now, and his words applied to more than my teeth. I had not caused the changes in my body any more than I alone had caused my marriage to crumble. I deserved to have my body and my life—a home, my children—back the way they had been.

But neither would ever be one hundred percent again.

Dr. Peterson, who put me back together, told me that one day my body would be normal again, but only ninety percent. I would never be *completely* normal again.

And even if I had my own home one day, I had come to realize that my children would never live with me again. Sure, they would come stay with me, and yes, they would always need their mother, but the bedrooms of my children—where they slept every night— were in what was now their father's house. A place they had called home for thirteen years, and for Connor, all of his life.

I held in my tears and smiled a toothless smile.

Implants. Two new teeth.

In the meantime, the gap in the front of my mouth would be filled with a removable partial denture the dentist called a "flipper," which I would wear while my gums healed and until the brand-new teeth were in place. My flipper would come back from the lab two weeks later and fit the spot perfectly while I awaited my new teeth. Unless you looked closely or noticed the thickness of my speech, you would never know it was fake.

That flipper would restore some of my confidence, and I wore it for more than a year. My broken smile was fixed! True, it was temporary and removable, and no, it wasn't the award-winning best smile in the LHS Class of '87, but it was still mine. (Those commercials for dental centers that promise a brand-new smile in just one day because of same-day dental implants have to be lying or not doing something correctly, because it certainly was nothing like that in my case.)

Fourteen months later, after the implants and crowns were completely in place, I would peer into the dentist's hand mirror and notice something very interesting: Not only did both teeth fill their spots well, but my new front tooth was whiter, smoother, and better than the old one. It was perfect. Maybe even more beautiful than before. Finally, my smile was back!

When I returned home that day, I took the flipper out of the pocket of my purse and held it in the palm of my hand. *What should I do with it?* I wanted to throw it away and never lay eyes on it again, but I was afraid to. It had been my vanity's safeguard, a friend who filled a void. A void I never wanted to feel again. I decided to keep it just in case.

I pulled a Ziploc baggie from the kitchen drawer, placed the mouthpiece inside, and smoothed the closure with my fingers. I put it inside the bathroom's mirrored medicine cabinet on a shelf and closed the door. I knew I would keep the flipper forever, and for so many, many reasons.

I leaned in to the mirror as close as I could and bared my front teeth. Ah, yes. My front tooth was back. And it was pretty. *I* was pretty.

I smiled at Aimee.

I could tell from her reflection that it felt good to have a secure smile in place again, because she was beaming back at me.

2000 and Beyond

When students found out about my Ricky Martin love affair, they started bringing in anything Ricky they could find, and soon my modest Ricky photo collection outgrew the insides of a book cabinet's metal doors where it started, spilling posters, calendars, cards, and stickers all over my classroom walls.

Students added to it regularly, eventually growing it to behemoth proportions. They even nicknamed it "The Ricky Shrine."

And I loved that. I loved him.

"If we ever walk in and candles are lit, we're calling the men in white coats to take you away," my students joked.

"Go ahead," I replied.

"Choose: your husband or Ricky," students teased.

"Nah, I can't," I replied.

"He's probably gay," students said.

"So what," I replied.

For more than sixteen years, Ricky was a permanent fixture of Room 110—he was maybe even my co-teacher. We—Ricky and I—were a lot alike. He's a proud humanitarian who built houses for Habitat for Humanity after earthquakes in Thailand, Haiti, and Chile, and I was a proud educator, confident of my efforts to teach students and other teachers nationwide about the Holocaust.

As Ricky transformed from Latin heartthrob to one of the best-known child-welfare humanitarians in the Third World, even creating his own foundation, I traveled to Germany and Poland, became a regional educator for the United States Holocaust Memorial Museum, and shared resources across the nation with other educators.

In a 2010 CNN interview about his philanthropic work for the Ricky Martin Foundation, Ricky said, "Heroes represent the best of ourselves, respecting that we are human beings. A hero can be anyone from Gandhi to your classroom teacher, anyone who can show courage when faced with a problem. A hero is someone who is willing to help others in his or her best capacity. It can be someone teaching another to write, saving someone in danger, or giving up your life for another."

And I loved that. I loved him.

Then, while writing his autobiography, *Me*, Ricky came out publicly as a proud homosexual man.

"Did you know he's gay?" students asked. As if that mattered.

"Did you know his grandmother was a professor who wrote a couple of books, and his great-grandmother was a teacher?" I asked them. Kind of like me and my aspirations.

As time passed, though, students no longer knew who Ricky Martin was.

"Who's *that* guy?" they asked, pointing at his posters or the life-size cut-out of him decorating my room.

And then I told them our story and how much we had in common, or I sang the lyrics to "Shake Your Bon-Bon," "She Bangs," or "Livin' La Vida Loca." Sometimes, I even showed them his music videos. I felt it was my cultural duty to educate them, after all.

And they loved it.

They loved that their middle-aged, goofy English instructor was "in love" with a gay Latino singer, or as they put it, "Totally crushing like a fangirl."

I supposed my crush made me unique in their eyes. It made me human.

In fact, I came to accept the fact that one day, after I have retired, after thirty-seven years or more of teaching Chaucer and Shakespeare, essay writing and literary analysis, vocabulary, annotation, and grammar, the indelible mark I will have left on education at Loudonville High School will be one of two ironically related things: my love of Ricky Martin or my passion for teaching about the Holocaust.

Unless a strange turn of events happens between now and then.

"What would you do if Ricky walked through your classroom door right now?" students would ask me.

"Oh my God, I would die," I always told them, totally crushing like a fangirl.

And I probably would.

Being home from the hospital continued to agree with me.

Jerrica, Natalie, and Connor stopped by every day after school, and any combination of the three came to hang out on the weekends. It was good to be near them again on a regular basis.

My physical progress and many firsts read like a laundry list of things normally taken for granted: appetite back, first outing, less pain medication needed, first time being left alone, slept through the night, first glass of chardonnay, able to groom herself, first shower (seven weeks to the day after the accident), and so on. After three weeks, I was out of the wheelchair and on crutches, and a few days later, I was taken off the wound vac.

My broken body was healing, improving every day, but my mind—my psychological state—was a mess. I was trying to come to terms with so many things.

I wondered what the limitations of my new body might mean to the future. I detested having my mother take care of me at my age. I worried about missing the start of the school year, especially Jerrica's senior year. I wanted a normal life again.

I questioned surviving the accident when the other driver did not, and I tried hard to wrap my mind around the fact that I had been resuscitated. *What was so special about me, but not him? Why was I still alive?*

Sometimes I thought of all the wounded people I had encountered in the hospital. My roommates: the girl whose boyfriend had tried to kill her with the car she was driving, the woman with the undiagnosed disease who had helped me to stop pitying myself, and the other roommate who had fallen from a ladder while painting a ceiling and landed on her back. The Hell's Angel who had lost half his leg.

I wondered what had happened to them. *Were they now "comebacks," too? Were they questioning still being alive? Were they even still alive?*

Chances were, I would never know.

Just like the things I would never know about Zach or the accident. It seemed like so much more than a random act in the Universe. It had to mean something to my life. Accidents are accidents because they are unfortunate incidents that happen unexpectedly and unintentionally. But this was no accident. Sure, it was unfortunate and unexpected, but there was intention. A young man of only nineteen years got into a car with the purpose of driving it. Straight through a stop sign. At a high rate of speed. He made choices. He caused a tragic wreck, not an "accident."

Within a split second following his stupid decisions, he had wrecked my car, my body, and my life. And it didn't matter that he paid the ultimate sacrifice for his mistake. No, his death did not diminish my anger. Instead, my contempt just seemed to grow exponentially.

I hated him.

• • •

Gossip spreads quickly in a small town—everyone knows that—but it is especially true after a tragedy.

Visitors—old friends, colleagues, and former students—started to come by regularly, filling the time between rest and doctors' appointments. I needed the distraction, and I loved the company. Some were shocked by my injuries and appearance, unable to hide their tears. Some were overwhelmed with gratitude that I had survived. And some shared stories they'd heard about the young man who had plowed into us that night.

I heard he'd lost his license before, been in trouble with the law.

I heard he was a real party boy.

I heard he was quite a stoner. Yeah, known for smoking weed.

I heard he played driving games with his buddies, running stop signs and stuff for points. For fun.

I can't say I was surprised by the rumors, especially in our rural area where everyone knew someone who knew someone else who was involved in some way, but once I heard them, they stuck in my brain. It didn't matter whether they were true or not, I couldn't stop thinking about them.

When I told the girls what I had been hearing, they weren't surprised—they knew kids who partied with him.

"Just don't look at his Facebook page, Mom," Jerrica said.

"Yeah, Mom. *Not* a good idea," Natalie agreed.

But I did anyway. I had to know.

What a mistake. Rumors were one thing, visual proof quite another.

Not only did we have a lot of mutual "friends," but a couple of them had started a page in memoriam, asking others to share their favorite Zach memories. I couldn't tear my eyes away—I read every post and looked at every photograph. I was nauseated. Three obvious realities about him started to surface.

1. Zach had a lot of friends and family who loved him and missed him sorely. The sadness was palpable.

2. Zach smoked marijuana. Numerous photos showed him blowing smoke at the camera or at his friends. Many of the memories shared were of the intense parties he threw, the times he and his friends got "chill" by getting high.

3. Some of Zach's friends were my former students, kids I enjoyed in class, kids who partied with him. They were angry he was dead and outraged by the newspaper article about the accident, because it focused on me and the drill team girls who had been in my car. I was not only disgusted and disappointed that my students hung out with him, but I felt betrayed. He was the enemy, and they were on his side. Perhaps they even thought I had killed their friend.

But I didn't.

This was all his fault.

I wanted to scream at him. I wanted to shake him by the shoulders and say, "Look what you've done! How could you have been so irresponsible? Were you high that night, too?"

But I couldn't.

He was dead.

• • •

One weekend, I asked Mom to help me get a few things from my classroom so I could work from home. I had been teaching at LHS for almost twenty years, but this would be Mom's first visit to Room 110.

Even though I hadn't yet returned, the room was still mine, according to the old paper placard reading, "Mrs. Aimee Young." I turned the key in the lock, grasped the metal knob with both hands, and yanked as hard as I could. The door swelled in any kind of humidity, no matter the season, but I was used to it, especially after all these years, ten of them in this particular room.

I entered and breathed its familiar scent: a musty mix of heated floor wax, slate, and Pine-Sol. It was the smell of an old, comforting friend I'd known since high school. It reminded me of marching band, cheerleading, first loves, and high school dances. I graduated fourth in my class in this small, rural district: the same district that hired my father for his first year of teaching and then saw him retire thirty years of service later.

This was not just a school—or classroom—to me, it was home. And I missed being here.

I also missed being around teenagers.

Mom circled the room, taking everything in as I shuffled papers at my desk. She was quiet—almost too quiet—as if walking through a museum exhibit.

"You know what, Aim? I think this classroom was actually your father's when the high school first opened."

I froze, shocked.

"By the way, I love the Ricky collection—nice," she said, still walking around the room.

Wait, how would Mom know this had once been Dad's room? And what if it had been? Holy smokes! This could mean I've been teaching in the same room my father had christened so many years ago!

This room might have been his? *And* Mr. Matthews'? And now *mine*?

"Did you go to the new high school, Mom?"

"Oh yeah, I was a junior when it opened," she said. "And I'm sure of it now. This was definitely your dad's room. I had math with him in here. But you should ask him just to make sure."

Wait—what? I always thought Mom had Dad as a teacher when she was in *junior high*, not a junior in high school!

I giggled.

"Mom! I didn't know you had him when you were a junior! You were, what? Seventeen? I thought you always said that you were in junior high!"

"No, Aimee, *you* had him in junior high," she said and laughed.

"So then, if you started dating right after you graduated, wasn't it a scandal?"

LHS opened in 1963, a much different time. Plus, I knew teasing her would get her fired up.

"No, not at all! Geez, Aimee!" she exclaimed. "He was my math teacher, that's it!"

But still—my parents had met each other here! This room might have been the genesis of me!

"Okay, okay, okay," I said, but kept giggling. It didn't matter to me that she had Dad for a teacher, or how old either of them was when they started dating. They were twelve years apart in age, but they'd been married for more than forty years. Their relationship worked, whatever its beginnings.

What mattered to me was the fact that my father, someone I had looked up to since I was small, someone I wanted to be just like because he was a teacher, may have been *the first* teacher in this room, six years before I was born. This room held my origins. No wonder it had felt like home to me for more than a decade.

How cool would it be if this really were Dad's room? What a legacy! I thought.

But it would be a while before I would finally remember to ask him. (I have a terrible memory. I blame it on the accident.)

Years later: "Hey, Dad, did you teach at LHS when the building first opened?"

Mom, who was standing nearby at the time, smiled when she heard my question.

"Well, let's see," he said, putting an index finger to his chin and looking skyward, as if for the answer.

"That would have been about 1963, '64. Yes, yes, I did teach there."

"So, do you remember which classroom was yours?"

He laughed in that way he does, partially sighing while shaking his head, then said, "Oh, man, Aimee. That was so long ago."

Dad was in his late seventies.

"Please—can you *try* to remember?"

"Okay, let me draw a picture to help," he said, grabbing a nearby pencil and a used envelope from the kitchen counter. The drafting teacher in him always liked to see what he needed to figure out in writing. (Huh. The apple didn't fall far from the tree.)

"Well," he continued, looking at the paper, "there are three buildings on the campus, right?"

"No, actually there are four—"

"But one is the gym, correct?"

"Yes."

"Okay, so I was back in this building right here, Building One," he said. "And when you walked in, there was something to the left— the library, I think?"

"Yes, the library is just on the left inside the door. Go on— where was your room?"

He looked up at the ceiling again, as if trying to place himself in the building, and then said, "If you walked all the way down that hall and turned left, the first door on the right was mine."

What? I almost screamed. *That's my room!*

"Dad! You mean 110? Was that your room number?"

"I don't remember," he said. "I just know it was the first door on your right."

"Ohmygosh, Dad! That's my room!"

Mom, who'd been listening quietly this whole time, grinned slyly at me.

"Told ya," she muttered.

I looked at Dad, waiting for his reaction. Would he cry, overwhelmed with emotion and memory and pride? Or would he laugh, hug me, and excitedly ask to come visit? Maybe he'd even want to talk to my classes!

"Wow. That's pretty cool, Aim," he said.

And that's all he said. Clearly, I was far more impressed with this information than he.

"It was only my room for one year," he said shrugging, as if it didn't matter.

"Who cares, Dad? This is a big deal to me!"

He laughed again, in that same self-deprecating way, but I knew he was happy about my excitement. How many teachers could say they taught in the very same classroom their father did more than fifty years ago? The very same classroom where their parents might have met each other? The very same classroom that had meant so much for so long?

This room had cared for me, helped transform me, and provided strength. It had seen me at my best and my worst, in both my professional and personal lives, and it had always supported me. Almost like a parent.

This room had become my escape, and over time, a safe place away from the chaos of the world. One of permanence. No matter how much I or my life had changed over the years, my room did not. Just like a home.

Blessed by my very own father.

• • •

Mom went home on a Sunday in the middle of October 2010.

Her goodbye was a tight, hard hug that said what words could not: I had survived and she was thankful, but she was worried to leave me. She knew I had healed enough to be on my own, but she was afraid the kids would try to convince me to move back to their father's, or worse, that Kenny would. She was afraid I was too weak emotionally and mentally to protect myself, that I might give in. Or that the stress would cause another heart attack.

As a mother, I understood her fears, but as a woman, I knew I was stronger than that. Look what I had made it through, after all.

I fought back tears as we hugged and joked about the day she told doctors she would stay until I could literally stand and kick her out the door. I finally could, so it was time. I just didn't want her to see me upset. If she did, she might not leave.

And I needed her to go.

I wanted to take care of myself again; in fact, I yearned for some sort of normalcy to return to my life, though I really hadn't had the chance to find that place yet. I had been living in the Victorian for only two months, our divorce final only a month, when the accident happened. It was taking so long to be me, new and fresh and on my own, and now I could, because Mom was leaving.

She laughed, and we said our goodbyes. I waved as her Honda SUV pulled away from the curb, and then I closed the heavy wooden front door until it snapped shut. I turned and leaned against it, and the tears I had been holding back flowed freely.

I was alone. On my own.

And I was scared. Scared to be independent, scared of my own fragility.

Without someone to protect me around the clock, I was sure something bad, something worse, would happen to me. If a car could shoot out of the darkness and smash me to pieces, then meteors could fall from the sky and crush me into the ground, or a roof could collapse and smother me under its weight.

Life could change, or even end, in a moment. That's just the way it was.

I could either hide in fear and avoidance or I could attempt to live with courage, one challenge at a time. And I was starting to get pretty good at that.

In fact, I probably could have won an award for it by then.

I circled the tables, collecting and sorting leftover handouts from the day's Holocaust education workshop I had just led, when I heard a woman behind me.

"Excuse me, Aimee?" she said.

The room had cleared except for a few people on the periphery, talking and looking at resources.

"Yes?"

I turned, smiling, still on the post-workshop adrenaline high that accompanied a job well done, and found a middle-aged face, surrounded by loose and frizzy dark curls, pinched in a frown.

"You know, you or the museum should really research the area you're going into a little more," she said. "I teach at a Jewish day school here in the Bay Area, and we have no trouble getting Holocaust survivors in the classroom."

I was in San Francisco, brought there by the United States Holocaust Memorial Museum as a team member for the Northern California Forum on Holocaust Education. We had split into five separate classroom sessions to accommodate more than 200 attendees, including survivors, and this woman had been in mine. We'd just wrapped up a few days of sharing resources and strategies for teaching about the Holocaust, which included finding survivor testimony.

I wondered how I should respond. I didn't want to speak on behalf of the museum, because it wasn't my place. And I had been trying to help teachers who might not have access to bringing survivors into their classroom.

"Also—" she continued.

I tensed. *Uh oh.* The soft fluorescent lights overhead reflected in her wire-framed, circular glasses.

"You made it very clear that you are from a small, rural town and that you are not Jewish."

"Yes," I agreed.

"So, what right do you think you have to teach about this?" she accused.

During the course of the workshop, I had shared that I taught high school English at my alma mater and that I lived in the same small town where I grew up—with little to no diversity—and yes, I had also shared I was not Jewish. *But why did any of that matter?* I was just giving my audience the context necessary to understand my pedagogy.

I felt the heat of blood rush into my cheeks as a tight pain crossed my forehead.

It's a good thing I hadn't told them how I'd gotten my start in Holocaust education!

At first, it was about money and convenience. After just two years of teaching, I found out that I needed only a few more semester hours to move up a level on the district's salary scale. When I saw that a weeklong course on teaching the Holocaust was being offered at a nearby university during my summer vacation, I was intrigued, and I was sure it would be easy to schedule a sitter for my then one- and three-year-old daughters.

It turned out that the course was more than intriguing. It changed me.

For that week, every day and all day long, I was immersed in Holocaust history, documentaries, literature, writing, and speakers. The more I learned, the more horrified I became. *How could people treat other human beings like that? And how was it possible that children could be separated from their mothers or fathers or families?* As a new and young mother, I was appalled. I knew then that I had to teach about this tragic time period to connect students to the most important lesson that anyone can ultimately learn: We are all human beings sharing the same world, no better than anyone else.

That's what right I had.

But my brain was too slow catching up to her criticism to respond, and she had made her point. She was gone. Hot tears formed behind my eyes, threatening to spill, but someone was still in the room. I couldn't cry—not yet.

Pull it together, Aimee, I told myself, continuing to collect the remains of the workshop.

She had no idea what I had done the past nine years, searching out any and all chances to learn about the Holocaust. She didn't know I'd raised over $2,000 for a study trip to Poland and Israel that kept me away from my two small daughters for almost a month. She didn't know that I'd developed my own elective course on the Holocaust, or that I had been receiving hate mail from Holocaust deniers for the past seven years. She didn't know I'd won a contest through the museum for a lesson I'd created to teach about pre-War Jewish life in Europe. She didn't know that lesson was filmed for an online video and published in a museum teacher resource. She didn't know that I was preparing to take a second field trip with students to Washington, D.C., that spring, specifically to visit the Holocaust museum and hear a survivor speak. And she didn't know I'd written and won a grant to bring a Holocaust survivor to Loudonville in the next month.

Man, why hadn't I thought of all that a few minutes ago?

"Aimee?" a male voice said behind me.

Oh no. More disapproval?

A younger teacher approached, smiling.

"I hope your students realize how lucky they are to have such a creative and passionate teacher as you," he said, before shaking my hand and leaving the room.

I was incredulous.

Two evaluations, each at different ends of the spectrum, both in the span of less than five minutes. I wondered if he'd heard her and just wanted to make me feel better. I wondered if he meant what he had said. And I knew which of the two should influence me, no matter the motive, but criticism tends to leave more of a mark, doesn't it?

And that's why I broke out in tears packing up the rest of my things.

Three days later and back in Ohio, when my phone rang and the caller ID said California, I winced. *Maybe I shouldn't answer,* I thought.

"Is this Aimee?" a female voice asked.

Uh oh. Was this call going to echo the biting words from just days before, or was I just paranoid?

"Yes?"

"I'm calling to let you know that you have been chosen as one of thirty-nine teacher-winners from across the country to receive the Disney National Teaching Award this year. Congratulations!"

Oh. My. God. OhmyGod. OhmyGodohmyGodohmyGod.

Me! An award-winning teacher after only twelve years! Me! Out of more than 10,000 applications!

Something I'd dreamed of since college had come true!

But here's the best part:

The person who had nominated me for the Disney Award was a former high school history teacher who had not only won the award twelve years before but was also Jewish and currently making his career in Holocaust education at the national level. He had observed me teaching—both students and other educators— on several occasions. If he thought enough of my abilities for this recognition, and my application had actually won, then maybe I did have a right to teach about the Holocaust.

This atrocity had left its mark on me, a permanent one, and I had to teach about it. Even if I were from a small, rural town in Ohio. And even if I weren't Jewish.

Frizzy-haired, frown lady unfortunately had left a mark on me, too.

But I would rebound.

With a vengeance.

From my living room on that late, gray afternoon, I noticed a police car parked on the street outside the apartment. *Weird*, I thought. It hadn't been there a few minutes ago.

Almost immediately, I heard a knock at the front door. It was a state highway patrolman.

What had happened? Why was he here?

My heart fluttered, rising, and lodged itself at the back of my throat. I inhaled deeply to catch my breath and opened the door.

"Ms. Young?"

"Yes?"

"I was wondering if I could come in and speak to you for a few moments."

"Of course."

As I opened the door to welcome him inside, I suddenly remembered that I had never returned their call after the accident.

"Please, Officer, sit down."

The highway patrolman perched along the edge of my beige leather couch and leaned forward, elbows on knees, a clipboard in his hands. He was tall, and he looked uncomfortably out of place in my small living room. He cleared his throat then, dark eyebrows resting under his hat like two fuzzy caterpillars.

"I'm from the Ashland Highway Patrol Post, Ms. Young, and I'm here to talk to you about the accident you were involved in, back in July."

So that was it. The accident. It had been over four months.

"I never gave a statement. Is that what you need?"

"No, that's not why I'm here actually...but if you'd like to give your statement in writing, we can do that," he offered.

Hmmm. Why was he here if it wasn't for my version of the accident? I was confused.

"I'm here because toxicology reports came back for the other driver involved, and— "

Oh no.

I already knew what he was going to tell me.

He flipped a few papers back on the clipboard so he could read from one, and I wanted to plug my ears. I didn't want to hear this, I just wanted the whole thing to be over.

"—the other driver tested positive for marijuana...and..."

I knew it. I knew it.

Wait. He said "and." *There was more?*

"...uh..."

His dark brows furrowed, and he looked at the paper as if it were a puzzle.

"Benzo..."

He wasn't sure how to pronounce it.

"Um...Benzodiazepine," he said.

I wanted to see the word. I leaned forward, and he turned the clipboard around to show me.

"I've never heard of that before."

"Neither have I, actually," the officer replied.

Unbelievable. That *and* marijuana. I wondered how the combination of those drugs might affect someone.

"Since the other driver was under the influence, I have to inform you that you are now officially the victim of a crime," the officer said, "and you are entitled to certain rights as such."

Victim of a Crime: a new title to add to my otherwise prestigious collection. It would fit nicely up against Supermom, award-winning teacher, Ricky Martin fangirl, local "Holocaust lady," and heart attack survivor, wouldn't it?

He handed me a pamphlet about being a victim of a crime. *How could a pamphlet possibly help?* I wanted to ask. Why would knowing I was the victim of a crime and that I had certain rights matter now? It wouldn't. Nothing could change or fix or soothe what had happened nor what I now knew for a fact: *why* it had happened.

"I've heard so many rumors about him," I said.

"Well, now you know."

"Can I ask you a question?"

"Of course," he said.

"Do you know how fast he was going that night? I've never seen any reports."

He flipped through a few more pages of paperwork and finally gave up.

"I don't see it here anywhere, and I wasn't the officer who wrote the report. I wasn't there that night," the trooper explained.

"It's okay; I understand."

"You can always call the post and speak to the officer who was on call that night," he said. "He could tell you."

"Thank you. There was a voicemail on my phone after the accident from him, but I never returned the call. I forgot."

"You can give a statement now if you'd like," he offered.

The patrolman handed me the clipboard with a blank accident report on top to fill out.

"I was going about 55 mph south on Route 60 toward Loudonville, and out of my peripheral vision saw lights, and then it seemed there was an instantaneous crash, impact on my left-side door. I noticed immediately my front tooth and then there was a man talking to me outside my car. I couldn't respond," I wrote.

I handed the clipboard back to him, so he could read it.

"What injuries did you receive?" he asked.

As I told him, he recorded a list, raising his dark eyebrows in surprise.

"Well, you look like you're recovering nicely," he said. "You're a teacher, right?"

"I am, yes."

"Have you returned to work yet?" he asked.

"No, I'm going to wait until the new semester starts in January. I'm taking a little extra time off to make sure I'm ready."

"That's a good idea. And I know this isn't what you wanted to hear, but I hope it can bring you some peace," he said.

With that he stood up, tipped his hat in respect, and said, "Have a good night, ma'am."

I closed the door behind him.

Wow.

How could knowing bring me peace?

I thought back to my hospital bed in the Trauma Clinic and the unfinished threat I made. *I better not find out the driver of that car was drunk or high...*

Or what, Aimee? What are you going to do about it? What *can* you do about it?

Nothing. There was nothing I *could* do.

The other driver had broken the law. He was under the influence, just as I had suspected. I had the word of authorities, and they had toxicology reports. Concrete facts.

Things I couldn't change. Things that don't go away or bring peace, no matter how much I longed for them to. They just become a part of the experience, a part of me, forming another scar.

And what was one more?

Spring 2011

As my physical recovery from the accident improved, I found myself questioning what had happened to my life more and more, specifically the end of my marriage, which I had never really grieved. It felt as if everything had happened so quickly between the heart attack and car accident, with little time to process splitting from my husband and leaving my home.

Now that I had time to think about it, I wondered if I'd actually come out on the other side of a mid-life crisis. I was in my early forties, married to my high school sweetheart, and miserable in every aspect of my life (except being a mom). *Did other people feel this way?* I hoped I wasn't an anomaly. I hoped having a mid-life crisis was a real thing.

So I researched.

First, I looked up the actual definition for mid-life crisis. Google said it was "an emotional crisis of identity and self-confidence that can occur in early middle age." Yikes, that sounded a little like me, but I needed more proof to determine my case.

During my next round of investigation, I found statistics somewhere out there in Internet land that said only two percent of marriages are between high school sweethearts, and if they wait until at least age twenty-five to get married, seventy-eight percent of them will have a ten-year success rate. We were engaged at eighteen, married by twenty-two, and still together eighteen years later. I was astounded. We had actually beaten the odds, even as teenagers who hadn't even figured ourselves out yet.

At least I know I hadn't.

After more research, one study by *The Guardian*, based on 50,000 adults from Australia, Britain, and Germany, claimed that mid-life crises were real and that life satisfaction declined from early adulthood to its lowest point between the ages of forty to forty-two (before rising again to age seventy). Mid-life is considered stressful, and though it is also associated with parenthood, children had no effect on a mid-life crisis or its cause. And as if that weren't enough evidence, I also read on the *Huffington Post* that women were more likely to go through a mid-life crisis earlier than men—between the ages of thirty-five to forty-four.

Whoa. It all fit me perfectly. I was forty-one and had three children when it happened, and judging from the statistics, I wasn't the only woman to ever feel the way I had.

All of the research certainly provided a baseline against which to decide my plight, and I was almost convinced. Then I found the writing. My writing. The writing of some previous version of the Aimee who would later find herself sitting in front of a computer Googling mid-life crisis.

That's when I knew for certain.

Tucked into a folder of miscellaneous writings from the fall of 2008, just months before I turned forty, and only a year and a half before I left my marriage, I found a scrap of paper with this written on it:

Life is a continuum of chance and choices, decisions deliberate and random, and as shifts occur, we simply live, moment to moment and day to day. Where will time take me? Do I have to be the socially correct, morally acceptable wife and mother and teacher and role model or can I just be imperfect, sad, questioning, normal, and human Aimee? I don't understand. I don't know who to be. And I don't know how to figure it out. Who will guide me?

Those thoughts, bigger than my head could hold and spelled out in ink by my own hand, were the ultimate confirmation.

Self-diagnosis: mid-life crisis. It made so much sense. Evidently, I *had* lost myself.

And yet I'd made it through. So maybe it was time to consider forgiving myself. I certainly could use all the help that forgiven Aimee could provide right now.

• • •

Once upon a time, I was a pretty good teacher.

It was all I'd ever wanted to be.

(Well, I mean, besides Cinderella, but I understood pretty early in life that might be a bit hard to pull off.)

I had wanted only two things from life—to be a teacher and to find love—and not only had I failed at marriage, but my job recently had lost its luster, too. My ho-hum life bored me, and in the years leading up to the accident, I wondered if there was something more out there for me.

I never imagined being anything other than a teacher, though. I never had a Plan B. For me, it was teaching or nothing.

In fact, I probably wasn't even in kindergarten before I had my first classroom. My dad hung a black piece of slate as a chalkboard in our basement toy room so I could play "school," and I gathered stuffed animals and Barbies around it for lessons. I even filled the pages torn from Dad's old gradebooks with their made-up-student names. I wanted to be just like him.

Finishing college, I vowed to become that one teacher— the favorite—that every student loves. The fantastically creative, inspiring, and entertaining Best Teacher Ever.

And I did.

I won awards. I was granted fellowships to study and write. I joined networks, shared exemplary teaching and resources, and traveled to conferences in cities all over the country. I was even a contributing author to *Today I Made a Difference: A Collection of Inspirational Stories from America's Top Educators* (Adams Media, 2009).

Contributing author! A high school English teacher's dream!

But after almost two decades in a profession in which extrinsic rewards were rare, my head and arrogance swelled as my accomplishments accumulated. Soon, I believed that only I could do what I did. That other teachers should learn from me. That the field of education needed me.

And among all the accolades and trips, even as I found independence and confidence, I lost sight of what I loved most about teaching: my personal relationship with it. With my classroom. With my students.

It had lost its magic, so I stopped giving it my all. I stopped putting in the creativity and passion that I had in the past. All because I thought I deserved more.

Huh, interesting. Kind of like my marriage.

Maybe there was no such thing as happily ever after. Or maybe it was just a mid-life crisis. Either way, I had been putting on a front, sloughing away days that no longer glistened the way they used to. Days that felt like they belonged to jobs others complained about.

And I certainly didn't believe any longer in the hallowed, English-teacher inspiration I'd once hung above the chalkboard at the back of my classroom. "You are the author of your own life story," promised the skinny strip of green bubble letters outlined in neon pink.

What teacher-catalog bullshit. Eventually I would become a character in my own life, unsure of who *was* writing the story.

But even so, and much to my surprise, when I returned to school on January 18, 2011, against the better judgment of doctors and attorneys, I discovered that my classroom was just what I needed. I needed its therapy. I needed its community.

Instead of spending long days alone, thinking about what had happened to my life, I was back in my comfort zone surrounded by teenagers, once again fueled by their energy. Students didn't ask me about what had happened, because most of them knew, but they listened if I wanted to talk. And sometimes, their unfiltered and honest words or questions gave me just enough of a poke to shake me out of the anger and guilt I was holding on to.

They treated me gingerly, as if I could break at any moment, and some even seemed to be in awe of me. I talked with a lisp from the flipper still filling in for my knocked-out front tooth. I also walked with a limp and had visible scars on my arm and foot.

Regardless, I sat in a chair at the front of the room and relished in being alive and back in my classroom. I wrote alongside my students, expressing my feelings and fears and trauma, and I welcomed sharing the literature of Great Britain that I knew so well. Considering how to read it, how to analyze it. How to see life and the human experience reflected in its pages.

Soon, it was obvious that I hadn't given teaching enough credit the last few years, and I started to regain sight of why it had once been my passion. I fell in love with it again.

I needed my students now even more than they needed me.

• • •

Feeling back at home in my classroom, I filed papers and put books away, lost in the chatter of teenage girls, until I heard the choppy propellers of a helicopter.

Oh no. Life Flight.

It was just before prom, and local law enforcement officials were sponsoring a mock crash for our students. They had set up the wreck in the student parking lot where everyone would gather to watch the follow-up scene as if it had happened in real time.

But I refused to attend. I just couldn't do it, no matter the cause.

Sure, I understood the point, and yes, I believed in it. Early in my teaching career, I had even advised the LHS chapter of SADD— Students against Destructive Decisions (Students against Drunk Driving back then)—and had students sign the Prom Promise for an alcohol-free evening.

But the trauma of our own crash, very real and not even ten months old, was all too fresh. So I opened my classroom as a place of refuge for the girls who were with me that night. We didn't need to re-experience it.

The noise of the helicopter moved closer and grew louder while we questioned and vented—*Whose idea was this mock crash? How could they do it so soon?*—but eventually our discussion turned to normal "girl talk" and gossip.

I wondered what kind of impact this mock crash was having on the rest of its audience. Yes, it was probably a short-term deterrent— *I mean, how could it not be?*—but at the same time, as I had just witnessed with these girls, teenagers were teenagers. Indestructible and immortal. Unbreakable. And kids forget.

According to the National Institute on Drug Abuse (NIDA), motor vehicle crashes are the leading cause of death among teenagers aged sixteen to nineteen, and the likelihood doubles when teens drive while under the influence. After alcohol, marijuana is the drug most often found in the blood of drivers involved in crashes, and in fact, drivers with THC in their blood are roughly twice as likely to be responsible for a deadly crash or killed than drivers who hadn't used. Recent statistics showed that in the past two weeks, one in eight high school seniors drove after marijuana use, and sixty-five percent of them were more likely to get into a car crash than those who didn't smoke.

But educational efforts like this mock crash usually focused only on drinking and driving. I just didn't understand.

We had become a part of the statistics. And so had Zach Ryder.

The truth was sobering.

One Year after the Accident

We think you should see a psychologist, Aimee.

The attorney's-office suggestion came at just the right time, and I realized my brother had connected me with caring people who could play more than one role in my life following the accident. I knew I should see a psychologist, too.

Just when my life was starting to get back on track again, five months after heartbreak, I had moved back to Loudonville, the relationships with my children were repairing, and...wham!

Yes, I survived the accident, but I was angry. I lost my smile. I lost my spleen. I lost myself. Other people made decisions for me, nursed me, paid my bills, killed my houseplants. The start of an independent, healthy life was gone, and there was nothing I could do about it.

Returning to my classroom seemed to be helping, but I had a strange new body and no self-confidence. I also couldn't forgive someone who had lost his own life.

Thankfully, my brother had connected me with an attorney friend of his to take care of financial details while I was still in the hospital. He specialized in personal injury awards, and his office was working toward a settlement with the other driver's insurance agency on my behalf. My medical bills from the night of the accident and the following month's stay were nothing short of astronomical.

It will help your settlement case if you're taking the steps necessary to get better, and we know what you've been through has been difficult.

I was still taking the Prozac my gynecologist had prescribed all those years ago for Pre-Menstrual Dysphoric Disorder, and it did take the edge off my assortment of emotions, but still.

Guilt. Anger. Extreme sadness. Self-pity. Poor self-image. And the never-ending anxiety.

The list was adding up, and when I took a hard look at my overall state, I knew I wasn't well. I knew these feelings were dangerous. Nervous-breakdown dangerous.

"Sometimes I just want to crawl into a hole, curl up into a ball, and die. But why?" I had written in my journal.

Like Alice, in a strange place she didn't understand, I shrank by the day, my only refuge Jerr, Nat, and Connor. And with them came more feelings of guilt. Not that they intended that, of course, but the feelings were there nonetheless.

It had been more than a year since I left my home (thus them, as well, or at least it felt like it), and I had still not gotten over this change, even though I saw them every day. I still had yet to grieve the end of my marriage. A heart attack followed by a car accident had decided for me that there simply wasn't time or energy for dealing with the fallout from my divorce. Instead, the circumstances dictated that I'd had to focus on survival.

A year after the accident, layer after layer of trauma had left me with wreckage I couldn't sift through. So many questions plagued my mind.

I wondered if I'd had a mid-life crisis. I wondered if I had been punished for ending my marriage. And still I could not find it in me to forgive the young man who'd done this to me. *If I couldn't forgive him, how would my children ever be able to forgive me? How would I ever be able to forgive myself?*

It was a vicious circle cycling toward infinity, this vortex carrying everything that hurt me. Painful memories, uprooted from their chronological sequence, flew around the storm's eye, flashing and howling at me ferociously, always sucking me toward the center. And when the storm wasn't raging, I felt hollow.

My spirit, crushed between major life-changing moments, had shattered into countless irretrievable pieces, spread across too much landscape to map.

I didn't know how to put myself back together without help.

Yes, I needed to see a psychologist.

• • •

Psychologist Number One: Interviews and inventories.

Why do you think you are here, Aimee?

Tell me about your father. What were you like as a child? How was it growing up with your mother? Did you ever experience any abuse—physical or sexual?

Do you drink alcohol? How much and how often? Has anyone ever expressed concern for your drinking?

Do you feel as if there's no point to your life? Do you ever relive the accident? Are you angry about the accident?

How do you feel about that? Have you ever thought about suicide? What's going through your mind right now?

The psychologist called me a few weeks later to finish our interview, and when I said I was having a horrible time with my memory, he suggested neuropsychological testing.

"It's possible that you sustained a head injury in the accident that wasn't caught, and testing can find that out," he explained. "I'll include a recommendation in your report."

Diagnosis Number One, Post-Traumatic Stress Disorder:

"Aimee is experiencing feelings of inferiority and difficulty with memory...possible head injury sustained...depression... great emotional sensitivity...angry, irritable, and edgy...afraid of driving...Aimee's greatest concern is that of her disfiguring scar... she will have to cope with anger about the accident and how it changed her life, the disfigurement of her body, and the impact of this on her body image and effects on issues of intimacy."

Recommendation: psychotherapy and neuropsychological testing.

I wasn't surprised by the report, just relieved with validation. A doctor had recognized that I needed further testing. Maybe I wasn't really losing it. Maybe I just needed some help.

Eighteen Months after the Accident

(Neuro) Psychologist Number Two: More interviews and tests— PTSD and depression inventories; IQ, Rorschach, and other memory tests; and tests for cognitive and physical reactions—ten hours' worth that spanned two days to determine if I had sustained brain trauma in the car accident.

Every time I heard myself say "I don't know" or "I can't remember," I felt more and more stupid. Throughout the testing, I never blamed the accident or young man who caused it, I just got angry with myself. He might have been responsible for messing up my body, but not my mind. I was in control of it. Or at least I wanted to be.

The results were less than surprising this time, too.

Diagnosis Number Two, pretty much the same as before:

"Aimee demonstrates a pattern of recovery that is consistent with recovery patterns of traumatic brain injury. She is also suffering from depression, as well as underlying anger and grief. She is guarded, anxious, and depressed, and she also suffers from social avoidance, left foot pain, memory problems, and suicidal ideation. She has feelings of powerlessness, and projective stories or drawings reveal an individual who is frustrated and overwhelmed. When faced with difficulty she wants to retreat. She also has some anger and guilt toward the driver who died."

Recommendation: psychotherapy and drug intervention for "neuroemotional" responses.

Traumatic brain injury. Well, I had suspected. My memory had turned to jelly, it seemed, especially my recent, short-term memory.

A second opinion, same diagnosis: I was broken. But this doctor's analysis also pointed out that recovery—I had sustained a closed-head brain injury—was happening and would continue with time. Slowly.

An extensive (and overwhelming, aligning with Diagnosis Number Two) list of psychotherapists in my area was provided, but none of the names was familiar, and I had no idea where to start. How do you choose a name from a lengthy list of unknown professionals knowing you will be sharing your innermost thoughts, talking about something you really don't want to, while exposing your soul? And all after a year and a half of way too many other medical appointments?

I didn't want to hop from doctor to doctor trying to find a fit.

So, I just didn't choose. I had every intention of getting to it at some point. I *would* seek out therapy eventually.

• • •

When the other driver's insurance company still hadn't offered a settlement amount, my attorney filed a lawsuit. A jury would figure it out.

I panicked. And then I cried. Maybe I did both at the same time.

Under no circumstances did I want to go to court. I begged him to work hard to settle before the trial date. I was anxious thinking about showing my scars. Maybe even more so about facing Zach's parents—they had lost their son, after all—until my lawyer promised he would do all he could to resolve it before then.

He reminded me that the county in which I lived was small and that I was a highly respected teacher who had taught in the area for almost twenty years. When I told him the presiding judge had been my divorce lawyer and the father of two former students of mine, he told me to breathe easy. Though this information wouldn't affect the case, he was sure it would make the opposing side cooperate more quickly, and he was right.

By spring 2012, the lawsuit hearing was postponed and a date for mediation was set. There would be no courtroom hearing at all. What a relief.

Meanwhile, I started writing again using the daily prompts given to my seniors in English class. I didn't write much, and I wasn't that great at it, but it was helping.

In fact, for the English teacher who also aspired to be a writer one day, it was turning into more than just a healthy hobby. When I found out that an area college offered a master's in creative writing, I was so excited, I signed up for the summer residency right away. I had always wanted to earn my master's, just not in education. This would be a perfect fit.

"What will you write about for your thesis?" Mom asked when I told her I was going back to grad school.

"The accident and what happened to me."

She looked puzzled and sounded almost angry when she asked, "Why in the world would you want to write about that when you lived it? You tell me all the time you don't want to talk about, so why relive it?"

Yes, I was sick of *telling* the story of what had happened to me.

I had repeated it to every doctor, every dentist, every psychologist, and every attorney I saw over a span of two years, and trust me, there were a lot.

It always got the same embarrassing reaction, too.

I was almost killed in a car accident. I was recovering from a heart attack that had happened five months earlier.

Disbelief: "Wow."

Yes, a heart attack. Yes, age forty-one. I know, crazy. It was stress. I had just told my husband of eighteen years that I wanted a divorce.

Pity: "That's horrible," or "I'm so sorry."

And then a shrug or pat on the hand with: "Well, you look great anyway."

I'd had two brushes with death, made it through the trifecta of shit, and I "looked great anyway."

So they said.

I never knew how to respond to that—*Thank you?*—so I just didn't say anything.

No one would understand anyway. My life had become a gloomy, tired documentary about trauma rehabilitation that most movie-goers would have walked out of, I was sure, and talking about it wasn't helping. I was just sharing the same clips over and over, and getting the same, unhelpful responses.

I knew I needed to make some sense of it all, though, because questions still haunted me: *What happened to me? Why am I still alive? And, who am I now?*

I resolved to do what I've always done when I wanted to organize my thoughts or solve a problem in my head. I would write about it. I could create a meaningful, enduring record of what happened to me *and* earn my master's at the same time. And maybe I'd find some peace in the process.

It couldn't hurt to try.

"And then her heart changed, or at least she understood it; and the
winter passed, and the sun shone upon her."
~J.R.R. Tolkien, *The Lord of the Rings*

※

※

※

※

※

※

※

※

We crossed paths one summer afternoon on a busy state route, just miles from my apartment, almost two years to the day of a different kind of crossing.

It was only a quick glance, a brief moment of recognition, but it was enough.

Jackson Ross.

We had been Facebook friends for eight months, acquaintances for almost twenty years. He had been a new student at LHS when I was a new teacher, and now we were both middle-aged and divorced.

"I think I passed you," he had messaged me the night after our cars had passed in opposite directions, sunshine providing a glimpse of each other behind windshields. "That smile!"

"It was me—I saw you!" I answered, intrigued.

Within the week, we had exchanged phone numbers, began a texting conversation, and agreed to meet for a drink sometime. The friendly banter—sweet, easy, and sometimes flirtatious—continued, and soon I realized he had potential, the timing was right, and this was not an opportunity I wanted to miss.

One night a couple of weeks later, during my master's residency, I asked him to join my new friends and me for a drink at a local pub. I was a summertime, sloppy T-shirt, sweat-stretched navy shorts, hair-wilted and make-up-melted mess, so I figured it was a good time to put our texting interest to test. If I could look like that and he showed up and stayed, then hey, maybe there *was* something between us!

"What's up?" Jackson greeted me, strangely raising his hand in a high-five, like we were old pals.

Uh-oh, I thought. *Who high-fives someone at the start of a possible date?*

And then I noticed his pale color-of-the-sky eyes and the way he looked at me when I talked. Our attraction was instant, the chemistry immediate, and the high-five became adorable.

When Jackson offered to drive me back to my parked car, I followed him and my heart, ditching my grad school friends for the rest of the evening. Once alone, it was only a matter of seconds until I felt his fingers on my cheek and his lips against mine.

Sigh.

We made out like teenagers, pausing only to move closer to each other, even giggling when I climbed the center console to sit on his lap.

And the rest, as they say, is history.

• • •

"Mom," I said into my BlackBerry, "I think I'm in love."

I was on a quick break from class, headed out in my nearly two-year-old Honda CRV to do some summer shopping.

"Aimee, you know it's never gonna happen with Ricky Martin, right?"

"Ha, ha, ha, very funny, Mom. I'm serious."

"Oh, really?" she replied, her words curling into an unseen but unmistakable grin.

"Yes! I've only known him for a few days—well, sorta, I'll explain—but he's wonderful!"

"Wow," she said. "What's his name?"

"Jackson. Isn't it perfect?" I sighed loudly in exaggeration. "I mean, Mom, could I have dreamed up a better one?"

She laughed, and I began to share our brief background.

I had known Jackson for years, and in fact, I could vaguely remember him as a student. This made my mom chuckle.

"How ironic," she said, referring to her own story of meeting Dad.

"But we're only eight and a half years apart."

And anyway, it didn't matter. Jackson had assured me that age was just a number, and that since it wasn't a ten-year age difference, I "technically" couldn't even be considered a cougar (confirmed by my own frantic research on the Internet). And I figured that since women live an average of ten years longer than men, I could be securing a partnership 'til death.

"Mom, he is soooooooo gorgeous. Wait until you meet him— blue eyes, tall, handsome, and he smells good *all* the time!"

She laughed again.

"So, you'll see him again soon?" Mom asked.

"Ooooh, I hope so—I really like him. This could be the real deal."

She laughed again.

"Now, Aimee, I know you are forty-three years old and a grown woman, but I'm still your mother," she lectured. "You need to go slow. There's no rush."

"I know, Ma, will do," I said. "Talk soon!"

• • •

Written in my notebook during the next week's residency:

Only two weeks and two days. How can it feel like this so soon?

Well, Aimee, you tell us. What does it feel like?

It feels like I'm falling in love. Not in like, or like a lot. In love. Hopelessly, madly, and passionately in love. A grown-up, mature "in love." *With an awareness that YES, YES, this is the one. Mine to love. Mine to want to love.*

It feels like those darn clichés about love—my heart skipping beats, finally finding the one, or when you know, you know—are actually happening to me, the cynical divorcée who no longer believed in fairy tales.

It feels like I've always imagined—unexplainable.

It feels like I could kiss him forever.

It only takes one, Aimee.

· · ·

When your very own Prince Charming sent you text messages like these—

Everything's so easy for us.

I keep thinking about looking in your eyes and smiling, and then I think, 'Damn, she is so beautiful, in all ways.'

Love when you wrinkle your nose.

It's your smile.

I'm probably the happiest man alive right now.

—you knew you better hang on to him. Like ever-after hang on. Jackson. *The One.* I could feel it. He *did* exist!

I was under his spell, enchanted over and over and over again on a daily—sometimes hourly—basis. My smile, with its brand-new teeth, returned along with my laugh—the one that wrinkled my nose—because of him.

He was real, and he was mine.

Jackson. Handsome, energetic, and charismatic. A self-titled "simple man," he worked hard and loved his two children even harder. Jackson's hobbies included cooking and watching gory old horror movies (thankfully, not at the same time), and he randomly sang bits and pieces to any song, from the '80s until now, like a human jukebox.

We shared a love of George Michael ("Don't tell anyone," he once whispered in my ear, swearing me to secrecy), and if I corrected his grammar, Jackson corrected me with raised eyebrows and a smile and said: "This is who I am—take it or leave it!"

He was comfortable, genuine, and silly—quite an inviting combination—and he made me laugh every day.

Jackson also made me feel attractive, sexy even, in spite of those ugly scars—the ones he brushed his fingertips against with empathy, the ones he wished had never happened. But Jackson also understood. Those scars had kept me from dying, giving me the chance to find him.

"Look, it's just something that happened to you," he told me. "I'm glad you're alive."

And I knew he meant it.

Jackson never treated me differently because of what I had been through, nor did he ask me to talk about it. He just accepted me.

Every time Jackson looked at me, he would say, "You're so beautiful."

And I knew he meant that, too.

• • •

Jackson has eight tattoos.

"Eight is enough," he says with a grin, but they are not an issue for me, neither turn-off nor turn-on. They're just a part of him.

He readily admitted that a few were crazy teenage/early twenties mistakes—the alien in a human uterus, the Buddha with back-to-back aliens behind it, and the creepy spider-looking tribal face—but his favorites were his children's names, one on each upper arm.

Jackson knew I had a tattoo, too, a sunflower, about the size of a 50-cent piece, near my right hipbone.

It was a badge of bravery from a years-ago, fun venture with my sister, an almost-dare. It sounded so exciting—and unlike me—to get a tattoo, so I did it.

A sunflower, symbol of warmth and happiness.

"Do you think you'd ever get another one?" Jackson asked. I just didn't know. I had enough permanent markings to last three lifetimes at least.

And then, after only weeks of dating, Jackson made an intriguing promise—another pinky swear, actually—to me.

"I'll tell you what," he started one night as we sat outside on his back deck.

"I'm so proud to know you, Aimee. You have a goal, and I believe in you. This book you're writing?" he went on. "I know you'll do it. That's something," he said, looking directly into my eyes.

That look. Like he could see right inside of me. It always made me blush and giggle.

"I'm so sure you'll write it, that I will have your name tattooed across *my ass cheek* when you get it published. I promise."

I erupted into loud laughter.

"Realllly?"

How I loved him already. He made me believe in me.

"Yes, really. It would be an autograph of sorts, right?" he asked, also chuckling, his blue eyes sparkling with equal parts mischief and admiration.

So I said yes and stuck out my pinky finger for him to grasp, and he did.

Tattoo number nine: all mine.

I liked that. I really liked that.

During the next two years, any time I complained about my grad degree and what was then an elusive "book," or whenever I struggled, sometimes threatening to give up and quit, frustrated and bummed by how difficult the task, Jackson would remind me of *the* promise. *Our* promise. The tattooed-ass-cheek pinky promise.

Which everyone knows you can't back out of.

Jackson had helped me start to feel like myself again on the inside, but I wanted the outside to match—at least more than it did then. I wanted that daily reminder corrected, lessened, and hopefully faded, so the memories, anger, and guilt could do the same.

I wanted my body opened back up, so I could get closure.

From the outside looking in. Oh, the irony.

But this time was my choice. I had control.

Scar revision, liposuction, and abdominoplasty: the requirements necessary to improve my abdomen, according to my plastic surgeon. Phew.

I'd had to wait a year from the initial consultation to make sure the scar and surrounding tissue had healed completely, but the doctor I'd been referred to was confident he could repair my scar in some way. I'd also had to wait until the settlement was reached, because part of it was paying for the surgery, which was now scheduled within the month.

I worried—about the surgery, about the pain, about the recovery—and I almost canceled. I knew this surgery really wouldn't *remove* the scar, because scarring is the only way skin can heal. (Skin is a seamless organ, and when it is wounded, a scar forms. It can fade, be covered up, or be surgically altered, but it never *goes away*.) In fact, because of the tummy tuck, I would be adding another scar—one less remarkable—to a belly with enough already.

Would this really be worth it after all I had been through? What if

I didn't wake up? Or what if there were complications? What if my belly looked worse? (That wasn't really possible, though—my scar was nothing short of grotesque.)

Then again, I didn't want to regret *not* having the surgery, either.

I was torn. And afraid.

But I needed to do it. I needed a boost of confidence. I needed some peace of mind.

And those things were far more important than being frightened.

Before I knew it, I was standing naked in the coldest room ever, in front of strangers and the largest mirror ever, my torso covered with black Sharpie marks, etchings that magnified the flaws of my scarred front.

It was time.

• • •

My first post-surgery checkup, one week after plastic surgery.

The swelling was down, the soreness was diminishing, and I wanted to see what my mid-section looked like.

I mean, I *really* wanted to see.

The nurse helped me take off my shirt and lie back on the examination table. She removed the compression wrap Velcroed around my middle and gently lifted the gauze pad covering my new scars.

"The doctor will be right in."

She smiled, then closed the door.

I looked down at my belly. I *had* to see it.

I wouldn't mess anything up, I just wanted to peek.

I leaned up and propped myself on my left elbow, while I pinched the edge of the non-stick pad with my other thumb and index finger and gently picked it up. It pulled away without tugging or pain.

"Oh my *God*."

I whispered the words aloud in the empty space of the examination room.

Was that really *my* belly?

I was in awe. Astounded.

The horrific, pink, stretchy skin splitting the mountainous fat of my stomach was gone. The fat was gone, too. My belly button was gone, and my tattoo—whoa—where was my tattoo?

That ten-year-old sunflower, supposedly everlasting and permanent, was missing.

The plastic surgeon must have removed it instead of worrying about trying to save it. I pictured it now, that flowered patch of skin, lying among the removed folds of fat and scar tissue, remnants of my old self, piled on a sterile steel surgical table. It must have looked ridiculous.

But the tattoo didn't matter anymore. It was gone, just like that ugly, horrific scar. It was a part of my old abdomen, my old life, and my old self. It was gone, just like the former Aimee was. The Aimee before the accident.

I couldn't stop staring at my stomach.

Every day for the previous two years—730 days—I'd had to see that horrible reminder of the night my life changed forever. That's 730 times—maybe more—I'd had to think about the scar and what it symbolized.

But now I wanted to look. Now I was amazed.

The plastic surgeon had done what others said they couldn't: He had revised the lumpy, raw scar gaping across my belly into a smooth, flesh-colored, skinny seam running the length of my new abdomen.

The pink seam was unexpectedly and delicately beautiful.

It joined a new scar now, one from hip to hip, and together they formed what looked like an anchor: the steadfast support I would need for the old scar to transform into a memory, to become the history of my story.

This permanent mark on my abdomen was the seal of a clean slate, a promise for peace of mind and an improved body.

One for which I would always be grateful.

I stood in the kitchen of my new home and unwrapped the foil of a Dove Dark Chocolate Promise. I popped it into my mouth.

Mmmmmmmmm.

As the sweet, chocolaty goodness melted in my mouth, I looked at the foil's interior-printed "promise," Dove's attempt at a fortune-cookie surprise.

You are exactly where you are supposed to be, it read.

I smiled. How fitting. Yes, I was.

I sensed Jackson behind me and then felt his lips against the back of my neck. His neatly trimmed beard tickled, and I giggled. He wove his arms through mine, encircling me, and gently placed his hands on my belly.

"I love you," he said into my hair. "I thank God every day for you."

I loved him, too.

In fact, the more I had gotten to know Jackson, the more I knew I couldn't live without him. So when we found the most wonderful house and property on the same busy state route where we had crossed paths that warm summer day, we knew it had to be our home.

Another case of love at first sight.

"Mom," Jerrica said from the dining room the day we went to see it, "this house is so *you.*"

Sunlight streamed in through the sliding-glass door and accompanying bay window overlooking the backyard and the tree line beyond. It reminded me of the two acres between cow pastures where I had grown up.

Our home. A lovely, solid construction neatly tucked between cornfields and hills on almost three acres, beside a creek just as long. A place where I could immerse myself in nature and grow a vegetable garden and tend to flowerbeds and feed blue jays. A place where I could watch the sun set from white wicker furniture while enjoying a glass of wine on my front porch. A place where my children could crash on the sofa anytime they wanted or play whiffle ball in the backyard or throw a New Year's Eve party. An enchanting place, *our* new home.

Somewhere I could feel settled and whole and normal again. I had found my heart's desire.

I tried to hide the tears filling my eyes, but Jerr noticed.

"Mom, don't cry," she said while laughing. "It's such a good, happy thing."

Jackson felt it, too.

"This is it, honey," he told me. "It feels right."

Not long after we moved in, with work boots on his feet and a chainsaw in his hands, Jackson carved an "A" and a "J" in two trees at the front of the property because their roots were intertwined. What a romantic.

Dream home. Dream man. Perfect.

• • •

"Let me see your teeth," Jackson said leaning forward. "Smile."

Smiling for Jackson was second nature by now and almost constant. We were out to eat, and I had just cracked open a crab leg with my teeth.

I bared my teeth, wondering what he might say next to get a giggle, and then I noticed him, face tilted, eyes examining my mouth.

He waved his hand in front of his own mouth, and squinted in the restaurant's evening light intently. A look of recognition passed over his face.

"Honey, please don't freak out," he started, "but..."

Instinctively, I moved my hand up in front of my lips. The beautiful new tooth that replaced the one I lost in the accident had recently celebrated its first birthday in my mouth. I must have had a piece of broccoli stuck between my new front tooth and its neighbor.

"What's wrong?" The dentist had assured me that nothing would ever loosen that implant, but I worried.

"It looks like you broke your front tooth on that crab leg," he said.

I felt immediate hot tears behind my eyes. My breath caught and my heart raced.

I ran my tongue along the bottoms of my front teeth to see which one it was.

Oh, thank God! It was *not* my new front tooth.

But its front neighbor was missing a corner, a large piece, and it felt jagged and sharp.

"Oh no. What does it look like?"

I looked quickly to my left and right, worried that people would notice and see that I was fighting back tears. I had learned to be very self-conscious of my smile.

"It's just a small piece missing; you can barely tell," Jackson assured me. "It'll be easy to fix, hon."

I had to see. I grabbed my purse and reached inside for my makeup bag. I ripped the zipper back, and without even looking, found the mirror with my fingers. I held it to my mouth to see, while shrinking down into the restaurant's booth to hide from view.

It was probably an old filling that had cracked off, which meant it really *would* be easy to fix, but still. It was my front tooth, and it was a pointy, nasty looking fang right now.

Memories of headlights tearing out of the darkness and slamming into my car swirled around me—shock and fear—completely blocking out Jackson and those dining around us. The feeling of the other front tooth lying on my tongue. The embarrassment I felt for the way I looked without that tooth. The feeling of the "flipper" in my mouth, even when I slept. I didn't feel whole without my front tooth, and now half of the other one was missing.

I started to cry.

"Aimee, it's okay."

Jackson's voice brought me out of my momentary trance, and I looked at him.

"Baby, it's okay," he said again. "It's not that bad. Just call the dentist first thing Monday and go from there."

He was right. I couldn't do anything about it now, and it didn't hurt.

We left then, but I couldn't stop thinking about the accident. The breaking of my other front tooth had cracked open a wound that hadn't yet healed.

And I wanted to talk to Jackson about it.

"You know," I started, "I *know* there isn't *one* thing I could have done differently that night. It happened out of nowhere. I couldn't prevent it."

I had been saying this since the accident happened. Those headlights in the line of my left peripheral vision, the almost instant impact. I could not have swerved, braked, or sped up. Nothing would have mattered.

"So why are you still beating yourself up about it, then? Why can't you try to let it go?" Jackson asked.

"Because I'm *so* angry. Still."

I wanted to find forgiveness and closure, but it was taking so long. And I had a feeling that this was another one of those things—like a broken heart—that only time could heal.

"I understand," Jackson said gently. "But, baby, he's dead. You're alive. You're well, and your life is good."

He was right. I had thought these things, of course—my brain understood—but I always made excuses otherwise, self-pity at its finest. I had survived, I was still alive, and I had moved forward. I was also happy.

But for some reason, in someplace deep, down inside of me, my soul wouldn't let go entirely.

Yet.

Though a settlement already had been reached with the other driver's insurance company, worker's comp had not determined theirs yet.

More doctors, dentists, and psychologist appointments. Even more reports. And during one of those visits—almost three years post-accident—yet another psychologist (number four, I think), told me I still exhibited signs of PTSD.

As he questioned me, I heard my own words as if I were the doctor listening: "No, I don't talk about the accident. Yes, I still avoid driving by where the accident occurred. Yes, I'm angry. Yes, I feel guilt. Sometimes things irritate me or cause anxiety. I don't like the idea of traveling much anymore. Sometimes the idea of social situations bothers me."

"Why do you feel guilty, Aimee?" he asked.

Shit. Guilt.

I had said the word too quickly, but as soon as I did, I *knew* he would question it. He was a psychologist, after all.

"Because someone died. Because I couldn't protect the girls who were with me."

I hoped that was enough of an answer to get him talking again.

He didn't. He just kept writing, looking down at his paper. The pause was unbearable, but I could do it. I could wait it out.

When he finally lifted his eyes to me, he didn't speak. He just cocked his head to the side and stared, waiting. He wanted to hear more.

And I gave in.

"I feel guilty because I didn't die, and he did. I know the accident was his fault, but I don't know how or why I stayed alive."

I started to cry, and he moved a tissue box across the table toward me.

"Because medical professionals were able to save your life, Aimee."

I was off the hook. He had finally spoken, so I stopped there. I didn't feel like sharing the rest of the guilt I still hung onto. I couldn't.

Guilt for what my children must have gone through. Natalie told me she fell to her knees and hyperventilated when she found out it I was in the wreck. Jerrica was all the way in North Carolina—she must have been worried sick that whole drive home.

Guilt that this happened to me so soon after the divorce. Jerrica had just turned eighteen, and as the oldest child, that made her next of kin. She would have been the one to decide whether or not I stayed on life support. I just can't imagine my baby put in that position.

Guilt that Kenny had never gotten to come to the hospital to see me. I didn't think it was a good idea, because of the divorce and my family, but he was at the accident scene that night and spoke to me. He's the father of my children. I should have let him come.

Guilt because my mother dropped everything, including being with my father, to come take care of me for two and a half months.

Guilt because someone—a mother's boy, a father's son—died. A young man with his whole life ahead of him. If my car hadn't been in his path at that moment, maybe he could have sailed right through his bad decision with no deadly consequences.

All that guilt, newly stirred, circling inside and trying to settle. Yet again.

The appointment was over, because I was done talking.

"Are you currently in therapy, Aimee?" the psychologist asked. I didn't want to lie—it was obvious I still needed it.

"No, not yet. I have a list of providers, but honestly, I don't know how to choose. I don't want just anyone."

"I can help you out with that," he said. "I have a colleague, a woman, who deals with almost only PTSD patients. How about if we set up an appointment for you right now?"

I was surprised, thankful someone was stepping in to help me.

"Sure, that'd be great."

I left with an upcoming appointment on the calendar (psychologist number five, maybe) and a bit of a burden eased.

• • •

Psychotherapy didn't work.

At least not for me.

I tried it—I knew I had to—but forty-five minutes of a psychotherapist asking me question after question with none of her own input or thoughts got old fast. I left confused: *That* was psychotherapy? I had already asked myself the same questions she did while sitting at my desk putting pen to paper, fingers to keyboard, and I already knew the answers. In fact, I had them *in writing*.

What I wanted was help, and she didn't provide it.

So I canceled my next appointment.

One of the first psychologists who diagnosed me with PTSD told me that if not treated, PTSD would grow worse with time. Writing and analyzing my story must have been just the treatment I needed then, because I had been feeling better, not worse.

Better enough to decide against expensive therapy that did not feel worthwhile.

Instead, I would just keep writing.

• • •

Springtime: the symbolic season of renewal, rebirth, and hope. The color green prevails as motif, and April showers bring May flowers.

But on this warm spring afternoon, almost three years after the accident, May showers rained down on me when I got caught—just hours before a hair appointment—in an out-of-nowhere downpour. I knew there was a chance of rain, but the cotton-puff gray clouds didn't *look* like rain. I wanted to squeeze in a walk after school. I had been trying to exercise more regularly to shed winter's hibernation from my frame.

And I knew, based on my experience with weather and natural phenomena as portents, it had to mean something.

My first and only high school boyfriend broke up with me on a cold, rainy April afternoon. The tears I cried matched the streams of water running down the car's windows as Dad drove me home after the breakup.

I married that boyfriend five years later in a winter solstice ceremony as large December snowflakes fell, their lacy edges matching my white wedding dress. I had a heart attack eighteen years later in one of the last snowstorms of the season after telling that boyfriend-turned-husband I wanted a divorce. February's end of winter and a piece of my heart dying—both symbolic of the end of my marriage.

The dissolution was finalized on a sunshiny June morning, when I couldn't help but smell fresh-cut grass and think of a fresh new start, and I was in a fatal car accident as the summer sun set one July evening, the light of a young man's life also fading.

On this particular day, I had just crested the hill in front of the white house with the weird windmill sticking out of its roof when I heard the soft swoosh of rain sneaking up behind me as it swept across farmland fields. I smelled it, too, the muddled scent of wet dirt, almost metallic, sideways in the air.

I was almost home—at least it was within sight—when huge soaking dollops of rain caught up to me, pelting the left side of my head and my body—the side scarred from the blunt force of the accident, the side where my heart is located.

My hair was suddenly plastered to the left side of my face, stuck against the headphone bud in my ear. Drops of rain dripped into my eyelashes, clotting mascara and blurring the edges of my vision.

I realized that if I didn't act quickly, my iPhone was soon going to be water-damaged. I pulled on the front of my T-shirt, already suctioned against the whole of my back, to expose my bra and then shoved the phone down inside of the left cup. I put the shirt back in place, noticing that my shorts, hanging around my thighs at the start of the walk had now shrunk against my skin. The clinging, wet clothes made me feel naked. I felt exposed.

I started to run.

But I can't run, really. My rebuilt left foot has arthritis and two screws still in it, and I'll probably never even walk the same, much less run.

Still about five minutes away from home, I did my best hustle, jogging—but mostly walking fast—to get back to the house and out of the downpour. My home, now bleary and dreamy, just didn't seem to be getting any closer.

Weird. Time slowed down, I slowed down, when the rain hit me, and so I gave in. Why hurry? I was already drenched and dripping, and strangely, it felt good.

By the time I reached the garage, I understood it, this sign from the Universe. I grinned, pleased.

Finally.

Nature's tears had washed me clean, and now I could forgive myself. My children already had—it was obvious in hearing how they loved Jackson and in their encouragement toward my own happiness. It was time to resign the guilt I felt for the end of my marriage, a marriage I would still be in, unhappy with myself, had I not been what others might think was "selfish." It was time to let go and continue moving forward with Jackson, and this was the sign I'd needed.

Baptism in a spring downpour: There was no other way to explain what had just happened, especially to an English teacher who believed in the literary devices of life.

Maybe its symbolism could help me with the anger I still had about the accident. Maybe it would even help me find forgiveness for Zach.

I didn't want to be defined by those things, either.

I ran into the house and up the stairs to blow dry my soaking wet mop and change my clothes. It was almost time for my hair appointment.

• • •

As the flashback of the night of the accident, once a sharp and terrifying endless loop, started to fade into a fuzzy memory, I couldn't help but think of the crash as a story problem from high school physics, especially after visiting the site of the wreck.

A red Mini Cooper travels west at an unknown high rate of speed. A gray Saturn Aura moving south at 55 miles per hour is broadsided by the Mini Cooper when it runs a stop sign. Momentum propels both cars off the road and into a small field. Solve for the force of impact.

Solve. That's what I still needed to do. My body had recovered from suffering the force of impact, and my brain had come a long way, but some calculations still needed to be made.

The cross my mother had mentioned to me in my hospital bed still stood at that corner three years later.

Fifteen minutes from home. Almost there.

Though I had been past the site since the summer night he smashed into me and the girls, I had never stopped. I never wanted to be in the space long enough to think.

Until now.

I had been washed clean, I had finally forgiven myself, and now, I needed closure. Besides, something kept telling me to go there. I had to.

I drove there alone one mid-summer afternoon hoping for something—anything—to provide closure. Armed with my notebook and pen, I was ready to record my anticipated epiphany. I expected to cry, feel relief. I expected for the trauma to finally make sense.

As I approached the intersection from the county road and pulled up to the stop sign, there were road construction signs: "State Route Closed," "Detour." I parked across from the site. I had no intention of leaving my vehicle. It was a busy road, and from what I understood, Zach's home was nearby. I didn't want to be noticed. Instead, I would just be here, feel here.

Beyond the intersection, a cross made of two perpendicular skateboards—not beer boxes—jutted crookedly out of a grassy slope. The ground climbing from the ditch to the tilted cross was still scarred. Dry brown gashes in the earth, like my three-year-old wounds, littered the rise where energy from an inelastic collision was absorbed. The scars, evidence of an outside force. Inertia disrupted.

As I sat staring at the cross, I could almost picture my car, having just landed, airbags deployed, windshield shattered, driver's side crushed. I imagined what onlookers might have witnessed that July evening. A car shooting from the darkness and crashing into another. Impact in the intersection. Crunching metal, shattering glass. A body catapulted through the sunroof and against the unforgiving road. Momentum shoving the cars over a ditch and less than twenty feet apart. My smoking engine, four trapped inside mangled metal.

Natalie told me that she and another teammate had left the dance camp a few minutes after us. By the time they approached the scene, the road was already blocked by accident personnel.

"You can't go this way," a man told her. "There's been an accident. It's bad."

Meanwhile, my cell phone, lost somewhere in the wreckage, must have been ringing. Natalie wanted to warn me of the accident, the closed road. When I didn't answer, she called the other girls in the car, but they didn't respond, either.

Fifteen minutes later, as she turned into the driveway of her father's house, alarm set in.

Natalie jumped from the car screaming, "I think Mom's been in a bad accident!" Kenny ushered the girls into his own vehicle and raced to the chaotic scene flooded with light, engulfed in disembodied voices, and swarming with firemen, ambulances, and highway patrol.

But it was quiet here now. Bright sunshine, a gentle breeze, midsummer warmth. The perfect setting for something—anything—to offer understanding. Or forgiveness. Maybe even redemption. I was alive, but another mother's son never went home.

I waited.

Nothing happened.

I didn't even cry. I slid the pen back in my purse, tossed the notebook to the front passenger seat, and headed home. If only the intersection had been closed that night. If only we had taken another way home. If only he had been sober. If only he had stopped at the intersection's sign. Then we would not have had our paths crossed. T-boned. Crushed.

Four lives changed forever, another life lost. A cross marked the spot.

Almost like that story problem from high school physics, except this one was real. And it was mine to solve.

The force of two cars, colliding at 55 mph. The punching blow of one car hitting another, the impulse of impact rippling through both. Velocity, momentum, and energy absorbed from one car into the other, from both cars into the ground.

A lost pulse, spattered blood, splintered bones. Solve the equation to determine the force of impact.

According to the laws of physics, it takes less than a second for two objects set in motion by impact to come to a complete stop. *Less than* a second.

"One one thousand" measures a second.

Less than a second to see headlights, feel impact. Less than a second for a life to end.

Less than a second to alter the course of a life.

No matter how many times I tried to solve it differently, the outcome was always the same.

One one thousand.

• • •

A few weeks after I visited the crossroads, I wrote Zach a letter. Finally. When the words, containers of sorts, spilled onto the page, releasing all the pent-up emotions from inside to freely roam in a separate space, I felt relief. I felt the possibility of resolution. Finally.

The letter, self-intervention. And a way to digest all I had been trying to grasp.

Dear Zachary,

I'm writing this letter to you because I feel like I have to, even though I don't know you, and I never will. I can only know my version of you, an idea in my head, and to be honest, it's not a good one.

I know you were the driver of the red Mini Cooper who ploughed recklessly into the side of my 2008 gray Saturn Aura, oblivious to the stop sign that warm July night.

I know you were only nineteen, and not one of my former students.

I know you died the next day in a room across from mine in the Trauma Center after doctors declared you "brain dead." The impact of crunching, crushing metal had launched you through the sunroof of your father's car and onto the road.

After the accident, visitors told me rumors about you. They knew people you partied with. My two teenage daughters knew people you were friends with. They warned me of a Facebook memorial page.

I looked too soon.

You—the party boy with swag—were loved, and by many. They called you Zach. I wish that throwing bungers, getting baked, and blowing smoke at the camera didn't consume those posted memories and fuzzy photos.

A friend of your mother's told me you had been in trouble with the law, and I know your driver's license was suspended at least twice. At only 19, that's two times in less than three years. Now I wonder if other rumors I heard were true. That you spent time in a detention home. That you and your buddies played a very dangerous game earning points for traffic violations.

And then there's your family. Good people, I heard. I know you had dinner at home with them that evening. You asked your dad for the car, the one titled to him but given to you, so you could go to a friend's house. You were on your way when you crashed into us. I wonder if you brushed your mother's cheek with a goodbye kiss, yelled "Later, Dad!" and hopped through the front door, your older sister rolling her eyes at you one last time.

I know your family loved you. My brother told me your father and sister hugged him, moments after finding out you had passed, crying, hoping that I would pull through. I imagine that your mother was broken in a corner, lost in her own sea of tears. They had just been asked about donating your organs. I know your parents—an older, more settled couple—adopted you and your sister from another country far away. Maybe they couldn't have their own children. Now they can't even have you.

The most devastating thing I know about you, however, isn't that you ran a stop sign that night. It isn't that you were most likely speeding, either. What devastates me is that you were driving under the influence. The highway patrol officer who came to inform me I was the "victim of a crime" told me. They don't know how fast you were going, but they do know about the marijuana and benzodiazepine in your bloodstream.

Why did you do that, Zach? Why?

Did you smoke pot and do drugs so often you drove stoned all the time?

Did you forget you had family and friends who loved you, a whole life ahead of you?

Did you think you were invincible, maybe even above the law?

Three beautiful girls, teenagers on the dance team I advised, were riding with me on the way back from dance camp that evening. I couldn't protect them from you. You could have killed them. You almost killed me. Four more lives could have been lost. I believed my daughter, also on the team, had left ahead of us, but in fact, she was only moments behind in a different car. You could have killed her that night. The thought makes me sick.

I love her, just like your parents loved you. Our worst fear as parents happened to them: you didn't come home. They must miss you desperately. I imagine they didn't know about your regular drug use. I wonder if they were shocked, horrified maybe, to find out. Perhaps they have forgiven you by now. You were their only son.

But I am finding it difficult to do.

We all make mistakes and poor choices. I know this.

And if you had lived through the accident, maybe you would have apologized. You probably would have been sorry, too. If you had lived through the accident, maybe you even would have changed. You probably would have stopped being reckless, too.

But maybe your life ended because of how you chose to live it. Maybe change would not have been possible for you even if you had lived. I don't know.

I changed, but not by choice.

I am a different person today. Body, heart, and spirit.

I wonder what I would be like if it never happened.

But that's silly to consider, because it did.

You crashed into me.

I don't want to hate you. And I don't want to be so angry, still.

I even want to try to forgive you.

But I just can't yet.

Sincerely,

Aimee, the woman whose life you changed

During the fall of 2013, as I continued to write about the effects of the accident for my master's thesis, I realized I still had questions—mostly about that night.

In my quest for any answers the Internet could give me, I Googled the Ohio State Highway Patrol's website and found out that I could order the report from that night for a nominal fee. Of course, I had to.

It came in two parts: one, a PDF file I downloaded straight to my computer, the other, a CD burned with photographs that I'd received by mail.

The report shared nothing unusual: the date and times and names and vehicles of all involved, the weather and road conditions, the place of impact in the road, and the angles of the cars' trajectories.

And of course, I had seen pictures of the vehicles already—Dad took those in the days after the accident.

But I knew, pushing the CD into my laptop's drive, that *these* photographs would be much different. I steeled myself in preparation for what I already feared I might witness.

Altogether, seventy-five photographs made up two sets of pictures: one collection from that night, the other from the crash's investigation in the days after, where a summer shower had just passed through, leaving the roads covered with rain and wet enough to look unmarked, undisturbed...

But the ones from the night of the accident shared utter confusion.

One, two, three ambulances. A fire truck, a highway patrol car. Spotlights and gurneys and people in glow-in-the-dark vests—I counted more than thirty in just one photo—police, witnesses, firefighters, volunteer EMTs. A line of stopped cars and trucks only visible in the summer darkness by their headlights.

A Queen Ann's Lace blossom leaned against his wrecked Mini Cooper. The driver's-side window was partially rolled down but completely fogged up, the sunroof open, the rest of the windows cracked or missing. Now-deflated front airbags hung from the dash, and in the floorboard beneath, athletic shoes waited for the feet that had once worn them. Impact had scattered money, both bills and change, across the driver's seat and launched my front hubcap through shattered windows onto his backseat.

So much spilled blood, neon red under the cover of night, and other debris, indistinguishable, on the blackened road. A balled-up medical glove marked the location of another burst of blood, this smear staining the berm.

Smashed wildflowers encircled my demolished Saturn Aura, while more flowers pointed out the newly removed, cleanly peeled-back, tragic scars of the turf. The keys were in my ignition, which gave me pause, but not as much as seeing my earring, the one Jerr had handed to me in my hospital bed, lying on the blood-stained cushion of the twisted, mangled driver's seat. I wondered how much force was necessary to cause earrings to come out on their own. And in the backseat, against more bloody, blurred splotches, force had flopped Jorden's animal-print purse upside down.

Every image made my head ache, knotted up my stomach, made me cry. These were remembrances from a night I wished I could forget.

But one photo stood out. A camera had stopped time in the same moment that five firemen carried a stretcher away from my car. Two bare feet were visible at the end of that stretcher, one bloody from injury. Another group worked at the rear driver's-side window, which meant I had already been removed.

That stretcher was carrying me.

. . . .

"We go through bad stuff to learn things about ourselves," Jerrica once said to me. "I truly believe that."

Wise words from my first-born daughter, then in nursing school. They reminded me of the definition of existentialism I had written on my chalkboard for students after we had read Camus' *The Stranger*:

To exist means to suffer. And to live through that suffering, we find meaning in our lives.

Now I could see the book's lessons a different way; I could relate. I had lived through the suffering, and I was looking for meaning.

"I'm still trying to figure it all out," I told Jerr.

"Mom, your doctors didn't even know how you lived through the accident."

I shouldn't have been surprised, but I was.

"Really? Did they tell you that?"

I was aware that Jerrica had to sign all of my surgical consent paperwork, but she had never said much about it.

"Well, not in those words, but it was obvious," Jerr went on. "I think it was the second day after the accident, and one of the doctors was explaining the surgeries you needed. I asked him if you were going to be okay, and he wouldn't give me a straight answer."

Trauma doctors, who saw life-threatening injuries on a daily basis, were surprised I had lived through the accident. I thought of the voice in the car that night. I thought about the fact that I had been resuscitated.

And then, one winter snow day off from school, while writing at the kitchen table, I decided to look up "resuscitate" in the dictionary. *Maybe I was exaggerating its meaning. Or worse, maybe I didn't really even know what it meant,* I thought.

I sipped from my shiny black mug, then typed the word into Merriam Webster's website.

"Resuscitate."

Definitions: "being revived from apparent death or from unconsciousness." The word's Latin origins meant to reawaken, to rouse, and to put in motion.

That's what I thought.

I sipped from the mug again, wondering what synonyms the word resuscitate might have, so I typed it again, this time into thesaurus.com.

Raise again. Restore. Resurrect. Bring back to life. Breathe new life into.

Resurrect.

Breathe new life into.

Holy shit.

I knew I had been resuscitated that night after losing so much blood. I knew that trauma doctors were only "hopeful" I would recover. I knew that family members were not given the reassurances they needed. But now the idea that I had been resurrected gave me pause. I had never thought of it like that.

I'd been brought back to life. A new life breathed into me. A chance to start over. A chance to finally find the happiness and peace that had been missing even before the divorce, the heart attack, the accident. A handwritten scrap of paper confirmed it.

I'd just needed to figure it out for myself.

• • •

I left our delightful two-story house in the country at the typical time—a half hour before school—on a chilly, gray weekday morning typical of early April in Ohio. It wasn't dark, but the sun wasn't shining, either. Rain showers, typical of spring, had been predicted for the afternoon.

But today wasn't quite so typical.

I backed out of the garage and turned down the driveway, noticing the faintest specks of water, pinpoint-tiny droplets on my windshield, but only three or four. Not even enough to turn on the wipers. Not even enough to say it was raining. And certainly not enough to deflate the giddiness of my about-to-burst, happy heart.

Jackson wanted to marry me!

I reached the end of the drive, where I always waited to pull out. The slight hills hiding the oncoming traffic of the busy state route presented quite a challenge. In fact, if you were going to go, you had to commit.

Ah, the irony. *Was I ready to commit myself to someone again? And did I believe in marriage enough to try?*

I checked my hair in the rearview mirror and then glanced across the road to the field straight ahead of me, an open area before a tree line. I could not believe my eyes.

A single vertical rainbow stood straight up and down all by itself in that field.

I looked quickly to my left and right again to see if there were other witnesses, but no one else was around—no cars drove by, no neighbors stood in their yards, no joggers passed on their morning run. A rainbow for my eyes only.

A sign from the Universe that I couldn't deny. Approval. A blessing. A symbol of hope and a promise of the future.

Very strange, this out-of-nowhere rainbow, especially on a

morning with little rain and hardly any sunshine, the two ingredients normally needed to create such a phenomenon of light.

But not a coincidence. I understood this. I felt it in my heart and body and soul—all that had once been broken.

Its message was shining through.

• • •

Teenagers: the people with whom I have chosen to surround myself for seven hours a day, five days a week, thirty-six weeks a year, for most of the past two decades. You can do the math on that (I am an English teacher, after all), but I'd say that's a lot of time invested in the "future of tomorrow."

I'd also say it makes me somewhat of an expert on this age group.

Teenagers historically have been one of the most underestimated groups out there, but I've found that they really do care, and about lots and lots of things. They are also the most curious, honest, and open-minded group of people I know, and sometimes to a fault.

There's never a dull moment with teenagers around. They make everything interesting. They've made me laugh, they've hardly ever made me cry (except that first year—class of '95, you know who you are), and they've accepted me for me, on a daily basis.

Even with all my quirks.

"Don't rattle that wrapper; she'll flip out."

"That Ricky Martin poster of hers creeps me out for real."

"Dude, do *not* tell her you don't have a research topic today."

"What's with the word 'thusly'? Is that an English teacher thing?"

"Don't ever knock on her door and interrupt her while she's teaching, either. She will come unglued."

"And whatever you do, forget sniffling if you have a cold, tapping your pencil to help you concentrate, or crunching chips. Just not worth it, man."

They have me figured out, and they have for years—probably ever since I stepped into the classroom that first day. I have always tried to allow my students to see that I am only human, just like them, and they seem to appreciate it. Maybe even embrace it. I'm sure that watching me live with The Trifecta of Shit has helped students to realize it even more. And if I ever need my own personal cheerleaders, particularly with my sideline hobby of writing, I certainly know where to turn. Teenagers are my go-to…everything.

It just took losing my grip on the meaning of my life to figure that out. I had been so steeped in professional arrogance, thinking I deserved more, that I must have forgotten my ultimate teacher goal.

And that's where teenagers—my students—came in.

In the months, even years, after the accident and my return to teaching, students were the ones who helped me remember. As I continued teaching what I knew—literature and writing—I let my traumatized guard down, slowly, and resumed sharing myself as I had before.

Seniors in high school on the brink of the rest of their lives and adulthood, on the edge of true independence and adventure, those whose existence hasn't yet been marred by time or jaded by experiences—teenagers on the verge of *living*—listened to me, questioned me, thought for me and helped me process what had happened… to me.

They inspired me. My middle-aged self needed to hear what they had to say. I needed to see it through their youthful eyes.

• • •

I was in the middle of reading Darin Strauss's memoir *Half a Life* aloud to the seniors in my English class when their bullshit meters started to go off—at least the outspoken ones.

"You know, this dude's guilt is unbelievable," K.J. said. "It's, like, too much. Is he serious? Like, dude, quit wallowing already. It's not your fault!"

When Strauss was eighteen and a month from graduation, a classmate on a bike swerved in front of the car he was driving, which struck and killed her. His memoir was an attempt to work through the guilt and responsibility he felt for her death.

"Yeah, enough already," Corey said. "I kinda agree with K.J. on this one."

It was early spring, a couple months before graduation, when seniors were predictably skeptical of everything. I had hoped that this late in the semester a literary non-fiction unit, rather than *The Canterbury Tales* (a mistake I'd made my first year teaching seniors), would keep them engaged. I had also hoped that reading it *to* them, rather than assigning it, would help.

So far, so good.

"Don't you think you might feel guilty if you were in his situation?" I asked.

"Yeah, you guys," Samantha added, "you know you would."

"Well, yeah, of course," K.J. said with a hint of sarcasm. "But come on. He keeps going on and on and on about how guilty he feels. He didn't do anything wrong! Let it go, man!"

Quiet giggles erupted then, partially what K.J. had hoped to achieve. Students looked at me with wide eyes, trying to gauge my reaction.

Corey jumped back into the conversation then.

"You know, when you think about it, this book *is* pretty selfish," he said.

Selfish? Where was he going with this?

"He's taking what happened to her and writing about it, twisting it like it's his story, and guess what? He sells books," Corey said. "Selfish."

"Yeah," K.J. said. "Has he even written another book? Or is this the only one? Did he just write this one to profit off the accident?"

Uh-oh. This was not how I had hoped the discussion would go. Had I chosen the wrong piece of non-fiction writing for the unit? I had to get them back on track before they completely derailed the conversation. Luckily, I had done my teacher research.

"No, he has written other books," I said. "In fact, he started by writing fiction and realized he had to get this story out. The guilt was too strong."

I could identify with Strauss. I had only recently started processing in writing what had happened to me—The Trifecta of Shit—because I needed to understand it. I needed to figure out what it meant to me and the person I had become. And I also had gotten stuck in the guilt.

But I didn't want to talk about me right now. My story wasn't relevant.

"I know that if that happened to me, I would feel guilty," Morgan said. "I would need to talk about it, too. It must be so awful to know that someone died in an accident you were involved in."

"But it wasn't. His. Fault," K.J. insisted. "The girl rode her bike right in front of his car. He couldn't help it."

"You know, Ms. Young, this is just like what happened to you," Corey said.

I wasn't sure what he meant. I wrinkled my nose and furrowed my brows.

"Well, your accident, y'know…You did nothing wrong, and someone else died," he explained.

"Yes, but it was different," I said. "He was under the influence."

"But," Corey went on, "didn't you tell us once that you felt some guilt for what happened, even though you did nothing wrong? And you couldn't have avoided the accident?"

Oh, man. The discussion had just turned personal. Yes, I probably had shared that with the students. They knew I was writing about what happened, and sometimes I even shared my work with them. Modeling is a worthy educational tool.

"Yes, that's true, Corey," I said. "There is not one thing I could have done differently that night. It happened so fast. I never saw him coming. And yes, I do feel guilt. I couldn't protect the girls who were with me."

I hoped that was enough of a response. I also hoped I could get through this discussion without an emotional breakdown. I was still having trouble processing the recent events of my life on my own, let alone in front of students.

"Aw, but how could you protect them?" Samantha asked. "You had no idea. You did nothing wrong."

I no longer felt as if I were the teacher in this discussion, leading students to their own revelations and insights. The students were counseling me, and caught up in my own thoughts, I felt the words come tumbling out of my mouth.

"I also feel guilty because someone died. A mother's son. Someone's brother. So young. Sometimes I feel guilty because I didn't die. I know the accident was his fault, but I don't know how or why I stayed alive."

Alyssa raised her hand, and I nodded to her.

"You stayed alive to be here with us and to be with your own children. To keep teaching, to share your story, to inspire," she explained.

Wow. I smiled at her, blinking away tears.

"Thank you."

I was not going to cry.

"Yeah, she is so right," Corey agreed. "I think you have what they call 'survivor's guilt'? Where you made it through a horrible situation that someone else died in?"

"Yes, I suppose so, Corey. I have heard of that before. Hey, K.J., what do you think now? Does it make a little more sense? The guilt, the remorse, the sadness?"

"Yeah," K.J. said, "I suppose."

The serious tone of his words told me he was already thinking differently about the memoir.

"But the dude still needs to get over it! It was *not* his fault!"

The class erupted in laughter, releasing the tension our discussion had created. K.J. was good at knowing when to make a crack to lighten the mood, but I also sensed what he was trying to tell me. What the class was trying to tell me. In their polite and clear, not-so-subtle teenage way, they were telling me it was time to let go of my guilt. And coming from students about the same age as Strauss when he hit the girl on the bike, the same age as Zach who hit me, it might have been just what I needed.

• • •

Out of the corner of my eye, I saw someone raise her hand and motion me closer.

Kristyn.

Quiet and thoughtful, she was known by her classmates for being strong in her faith and mature beyond her years. Kristyn recently had gone through her own tragedy, losing her mother to a heart attack just days before school started last fall.

And now she was coming up with title ideas for her English teacher's trauma narrative. I had explained my thesis manuscript to students, asking them for their thoughts. Teenagers had way more creativity than I.

Kristyn continued to sketch in her art notebook as I approached her desk. Drawing helped her focus, and she did it quite often during class. She looked up and smiled at me.

"Have you ever heard of the Japanese artwork called kint-something?" she asked.

I had given students the key ideas and significant imagery of the manuscript to focus on—reparation, scars, shattered, etc.—and then let them brainstorm. Anything would help. I just needed a jump start.

"Um, no, I don't think so. What is it?"

"Oh shoot, I can't remember exactly. I mean, I know what it is, I just can't remember what it's called," she explained. "You should Google it. I think you might be interested in it."

"Okay, then I will—got any idea how to spell it?"

I had no idea even where to begin.

"Try Japanese plus art plus k-i-n-t and see what comes up," she said.

I was amazed at what Kristyn led me to.

The first entry to appear said *kintsugi* was a Japanese word meaning "golden joinery." It was an art form that repaired something broken with seams of gold so that the mended work was even more valuable than before it broke.

Oh, my goodness. Kristyn was on to something.

According to one ceramics website, it is believed that kintsugi originated in the fifteenth century when a Japanese shogun broke his favorite bowl and tried to have it repaired by sending it back to China. Metal staples were used, which displeased the shogun, so he hired Japanese craftsmen to find a better answer. Their solution was kintsugi.

The reparation with gold seams of something broken. An art form. More beautiful than before. Kintsugi as metaphor. Yes.

I had never thought of myself and what had happened like that, but it might work for me. My life had shattered into pieces, too many to count. I had become scar upon scar upon scar. Some had faded, some had been revised, and some served as reminders. All cracked and then repaired.

I had been put back together, literally—my doctor told me so. I had also been resuscitated—resurrected and given a chance at a new life, as I had recently realized. So what if my restoration embraced the flaws, even the ones I had tried to cover up? And what if my breakage became a part of my history, rather than being forgotten or avoided?

I was honored that Kristyn had thought of this for me. Humbled.

Repaired and restored, I was starting to feel whole again. Maybe, like that broken bowl, I could be better than new. More valuable. Perhaps even a more beautiful version of the person I had been.

My students thought so—at least one, anyway. Someone going through her own reconstruction.

And that was enough for me.

The classroom had become the perfect environment—without my realizing it—for a type of therapy to occur. And because my students believed in me, they were able to guide me back to myself.

It all made so much sense once I recognized what had occurred.

Teaching gave me a purpose to be alive when I couldn't understand why I was. Teaching provided the opportunity to share my story even while trying to make sense of it. Teaching and writing helped me beat PTSD while finding forgiveness and understanding for a young man whose entire life was ahead of him. Teaching allowed me to come full circle with the experience and to feel whole again.

My students, most around the same age of the young man who hit us that warm summer evening, did what doctors could not. They fixed what he had broken, and my wounds finally started to heal. They rescued me from danger and returned me to where I belonged.

Tragedies or trauma shouldn't define you; what gives you purpose should.

That was it. My new mantra. My own little answer to existentialism.

There are two versions of the story, depending on which of us you talk to. My version involves asking Jackson to marry me on a dreary April school night after we had planned our late-June Florida vacation. He claims he asked me sitting on our back deck in front of an early-spring fire.

But neither matters.

Especially on our wedding day.

Jackson's eyes, so honest and happy and full of love, matched the blue of the late-afternoon Caribbean sky as they looked into mine, moments before we promised to always find our home in each other's arms. I was the blushing—okay, maybe sun-burned—bride, giddy to have that moment, to have him, and to finally be one hundred percent, completely and undeniably, in love.

It was just the two of us at our barefoot-in-the-sand wedding, besides the officiant, but we were all we needed. We were all we would *ever* need.

Jackson. Sigh. What a gift. He lit up my life with a sunshiny-ness that was just him, and he made me laugh endlessly. Everything was so easy with Jackson—maybe because we were so much alike. He pushed me to be a better person, because he already believed I was that version of myself.

Our love—a true love—filled whatever emptiness had been there before, and I knew we were meant for each other. We took care of each other, and we understood how easily the love holding us together could break if not tended to regularly. It was a perfect love, though realistic and mature.

And it was about damn time.

Jackson's first kiss—from that night almost two years ago—marked me for life. I knew then I would be his forever. And when you know, you know.

So it only made sense that once our vows were said and wedding-on-the-beach-in-Key-West photographs taken, we'd hop on our scooter and ride off into the Florida sunset together for our own real-life happily ever after.

And that's just what we did.

August 2014

I swiped my key card and pulled the heavy brown metal door of the school building toward me. The vacuum created lifted my perfectly placed hair as I entered, and I wondered if the humidity of the non-air-conditioned, fifty-year-old building would be my hair's next saboteur.

I also wondered if my deodorant would hold out. The open house wouldn't start for another twenty minutes, and the building was nothing less than sweltering in the mid-August heat.

As I unlocked and opened the door to my classroom, I caught sight of the sheet just next to it, printed in bold, black font, announcing whose room this was. The secretary had remembered. *Mrs. Aimee Ross*, it said. My married name. For years, I had been called the other name—well-known in this small town—by students and parents and colleagues. For years, I had worked hard to earn recognition and titles and awards for that other name. And now, after almost a quarter century, it was different. My new name. So strange.

"Uh, Mrs. Ross?" the nasally pinched voice of a stuffed-up teen-aged boy asked.

I turned to see who had walked into the room, and I recognized him. He'd been in my study hall a few years back.

"Hi, Shawn," I said. "Looking for Room 110? You're in the right place."

He looked up from studying his schedule, his face an inch from the paper, and then with the push of a finger readjusted the glasses slipping down his nose.

"Oooooooh, it's still you," he said.

Still me. Ha! If he only knew.

I was nowhere close to being the me I had once been. The past four and a half years of my life had caused a metamorphosis of sorts, one in which, more than anything, I had gained a certain wisdom about life: It could not be controlled.

You could make your own choices, maybe even set goals or a direction, you could even try to guide it, but most of the time, that would be knocked out of your hands without any notice at all. Sometimes you could get that control back right away, but other times—in fact, a lot of the time—you just had to wait. And either way, you could control only yourself—your own actions and reactions—no one or nothing else's, because the reality is that life, no matter who's writing the story, just happens.

And it's short. Holy shit, is it short.

But whether you plow straight ahead or falter, you make your way through, dealing with whatever it is, being as strong as you can, taking one moment at a time. That's all you *can* do.

And here I was, back in the place I belonged, my second home, feeling more grounded and happier than I ever had before. My heart had mended, my body had healed, and my soul had finally settled.

No, I was definitely not "still me."

But Room 110's English teacher, no matter her name, was—technically.

I laughed.

"Yep, it's *still* me!" I said. "Were you confused?"

"Well, my schedule said I had this one teacher for English 12, but she was also my teacher in fifth grade. I thought maybe she moved up a few grades or something," he said and shrugged.

I laughed again. Teenagers: my people.

"Nope, it's still me, still my room," I said. "Just a different name."

"Ah, gotcha," Shawn said. "I just wanted to check. See you in a couple days!"

And with that, he was gone.

Shawn was my only visitor for open house that night, but that was okay.

The excitement of a brand-new school year with my brand-new name had filled the air of Room 110—the same old classroom it had always been—with a bit of electricity. The same old classroom where I would continue to make my permanent mark.

I *was* exactly where I was supposed to be.

And now—finally—I was exactly *who* I was supposed to be.

Yes, I was still the same old crazy English teacher/Holocaust lady/aspiring writer in love with Ricky Martin—I was still me.

But this me understood her breakage.

And this me embraced her flaws.

Because this me, more worn, more authentic, and more valuable, was illuminated with veins of gold.

"The world breaks everyone and afterward many are strong at the broken places."
~Ernest Hemingway, *A Farewell to Arms*

Epilogue

So.

It turns out that you *can* be the author of your own life story.

It also turns out that in writing your story, you could be providing yourself the therapy necessary to feel whole again.

According to Dr. James Pennebaker, a pioneer in studying the healing nature of writing, expressing what happened to you through words on a page allows you to organize and understand your experiences and yourself. This, in turn, provides a sense of control, something you most likely lacked during the traumatic event(s) that led you to need to heal in the first place. When the writer has given the traumatic experience a structure and meaning, not only are the emotions drawn from the experience more manageable, but the story most likely then has a resolution, or ending, which eases the trauma.

The process worked for me.

I am no longer a character in that old, sad story, defined by trauma, because writing healed me. Writing also gave voice to wisdom I'd gained: *Life can change, or even end, in a moment. That's just the way it is.* And you can *hide in fear and avoidance,* withering away until death, or you can *attempt to live with courage, one challenge* at a time, accepting each moment gracefully.

I came to redefine my trauma narrative as a healing one, hoping that others could take inspiration from me in some way.

I just never expected my mom would be the first.

• • •

"You're always so happy, Aimee," Mom says from her cornflower blue La-Z-Boy, a TV tray with toilet paper and potty chair to her right, a table lamp with *People* magazines and her iPhone on the left. "I want what you're having."

I am gathering Christmas ornaments and decorations the kids and I put up for her and Dad at Thanksgiving while chattering away about nothing to keep her mind busy. As I collect them, I lay them gently on the living room carpet so Mom can direct me to their correct storage boxes, even from her chair. Dad and Jackson are somewhere outside, taking down lights.

"You mean, Prozac?" I joke, and she laughs.

She needs to laugh. I know she is scared, depressed even, awaiting her next chemo treatment. Twenty years ago, she battled uterine cancer, but she's stayed cancer-free ever since, a miracle. Three months before Christmas, she was diagnosed with cancer again: Non-Hodgkin's Lymphoma.

"No, really, Mom," I insist. "The Prozac helps—you should talk to your doctor about it—but you know it's more than that for me."

I wink at her, and she grins back. We both know there is more to my happiness than Prozac, and his name is Jackson. Mom loves him, too.

"But how did you stay so positive during everything you went through?" she asks.

This takes me by surprise. Positive? That's not the way I remember it. Maybe because I was *living* it, not observing, like she was. Now, the roles are reversed, and Mom wants to draw strength from me, just as I had from her in the months after the accident. She needs inspiration. Maybe even a pep talk of sorts.

"You know, it's funny, Mom. I had someone ask me one time how it had felt fighting for my life, and I just didn't have a good answer. Same as now."

I continue wrapping fragile ornaments in paper and delicately placing them in their boxes while I mull over her question. Mom watches, calling out every so often which container goes with what decoration.

What a cop-out, I think. That's not what she wants to hear. Yes, the passage of time and self-reflection have given me perspective on my experiences, but how could what I had gone through help her? She had already beaten cancer once before.

But it's the least I can do for her now.

"I mean, at the time, I didn't know I was fighting for my life. I was just doing what everyone told me to do. I think it's the same with what you're asking me. I don't remember being positive, Mom. I can't lie. But no matter how much I didn't want it happening to me, and no matter how much I thought, 'This isn't the way my life is supposed to go,' it still did. And I just didn't see any other alternative than to deal with it as it came at me."

No real mystery, I guess, just life. And strength, I think, even though its source isn't always clear.

"Maybe it's having enough strength to see—to hope—beyond the moment?"

Mom sighs.

"Yeah," she says. "I guess you're right. I'm trying, Aimee. I really am."

And I know she is.

"It's just"—her voice breaks—"hard." She lowers her head into her hands, now crying through the fingertips framing her face, and says, "I don't want to die."

But I know she already is.

All I can say is, "I know, Mom. I know. No one does."

Five months later, when Mom initiates a conversation with me about mortality, I fold myself up beside her in bed and hold her hand. What's left of her hair, after months of intense chemotherapy, has turned into a patchwork of cottony soft tufts, and she can only lie in one position, her head against a pillow on her right side. Mostly she just listens during our "discussion," sometimes smiling, sometimes murmuring an "mmmmm-hmmmm" as I ramble on, not really sure of what to say. Time and grief have clouded the memory, but I think I tell her that when faced with death, I'd been okay with it. That I hadn't been afraid. I think I tell her she shouldn't be either. And I know I am stroking her arm, just like she often did for me, whether after the accident or ill as a child, to let me know that she was there.

We are quiet then, together but alone in that space, while a surreal awareness envelops us: Her death is imminent.

• • •

In the months after Mom's passing, I realize why I need to share my story—why *we* have to share *our* stories—with others. For understanding. For comfort.

Because others' stories not only help us to find meaning in our own chaos, they help us to understand our own emotions. Stories can even keep our loved ones alive—and with us—through our shared history or memories, because for those moments of retelling, time collapses, and the past can be present.

Mom was by my side during that very bad year of The Trifecta of Shit, helping me fight. Helping me to be strong. She witnessed my story. But in her final weeks, Mom wanted to know how I had made sense of it all. She wanted to know how to not be afraid. She wanted to know she was not alone.

Our relationship led to a significant shared connection, one that eased both of our pains. One that everyone deserves.

Mom helped me to live again, and then I helped her to die.

• • •

Mom's been gone just over a year.

"You are our miracle, Aimee," Dad still tells me—even though it's been seven years since my trauma—often enough to remind me that my loved ones remember my story and are thankful I'm still here. His words also remind me I wasn't alone when I faced my own mortality—not once, but twice—and lived to tell about it. In fact, lived to question it: Why *was* I still alive?

But now I know the answer to my question—finally.

My story—the one I need to share as part of the human collective—isn't over yet. Nor am I done saving others' stories to learn from either.

The stories of my children. My mom. My new husband and his family. My dad. My sister and her husband and their son. My brother and his wife and their three children. My friends, far and near.

My students and colleagues.

The relationships that are a part of my life's narrative.

Through them, I live. I thrive. We share attachments and connections—we share stories—which creates my very being. Nothing is more important.

Everyone has a story. All of us.

It's what we do with our stories—what we learn and how we share it—that matters. It's how we listen to each other, helping to fill the cracks and crevices of missing meaning for reparation. For healing. For shared understanding.

Storytelling is at the heart of the basic human condition, critical to what sets us apart as a life form. So, tell them. Listen to them. Help revise them again and again and again.

Until they provide answers. Until they feel right.

Until they leave a permanent mark.

Acknowledgments

Writing a book is hard. Especially when you have dedicated your life to teaching others to have respect for the written word. To have respect for the intricate ways writers weave together and communicate their stories. Especially when you want to get it just right. Each and every word.

This particular story was difficult to tell for many, many reasons. And yes, a story can have many sides, but this one is mine—*my* truth and what I remember, even after trauma and memory loss. This story is an effort to make sense of what happened to me during that horrible, bad year, so I can move forward. Most of the characters' (or locations') names have been changed—out of respect—unless permission was given.

Jerrica, Natalie, and Connor, thank you for giving me the understanding and support necessary to tell this story. I love you all so, so much.

Thank you, Mom, Dad, Tina, Brian, Heidi, and Bob, for visiting or taking care of me during the time after the accident, as well as filling the gaps for me when my memory failed later.

To Erin Wood, whom I hope to call *my* editor forever, I extend heartfelt gratitude. Your patience, ideas, recommendations, and love of the craft made this manuscript a book, and your intuitiveness and insight led to *Permanent Marker*'s actual completion.

I would also like to thank Jennifer Scroggins at KiCam Projects for her encouragement and help throughout the entire process.

A special thank you to Josette Kubaszyk for her special inspiration.

Thank you to the following early readers—all former students and one, also a colleague—Marissa Burd, Kari Reidenbach, Brennan Smith, Kirstie Swanson, and Caleb Westfall. Your reactions and suggestions shaped this story into what it is today.

Thank you to my therapists, Angela Steiner and Jill Karchella-Johnson, who keep me looking and feeling like a princess.

Thank you to my cheerleaders, those former and current students of mine from almost every year I taught—a lengthy quarter century—who believed in me when I said that someday I'd write my own book. Especially Paige.

And Jackson, thank you...for being my everything. (Your tattoo appointment has been scheduled.)

Bibliography

Camus, Albert, and Matthew Ward. *The Stranger*. A.A. Knopf, 2006.

Carroll, Lewis. *Alice's Adventures in Wonderland*. Penguin Classics, 2013.

Delistraty, Corey C. "The Psychological Comforts of Storytelling." *The Atlantic*, Atlantic Media.

Company, 2 Nov. 2014, www.theatlantic.com/health/archive/ 2014/11/the-psychological-comforts-of-storytelling/381964/.

Hemingway, Ernest. *A Farewell to Arms*. C. Scribner's Sons, 1990.

Palahniuk, Chuck. *Fight Club*. W.W. Norton & Co., 2005.

Pennebaker, James W., and Janel D. Seagal. "Forming a Story: The Health Benefits of Narrative." *Journal of Clinical Psychology*, vol. 55, no. 10, 1999, pp. 1243–1254., doi:10.1002/(sici)1097-4679 (199910)55:10<1243::aid-jclp6>3.0.co;2-n.

Strauss, Darin. *Half a Life: A Memoir*. Random House Trade Paperbacks, 2011.

Tolkien, J.R.R. *The Lord of the Rings*. Houghton Mifflin, 2005.

Underwood, Joseph W. *Today I Made a Difference: A Collection of Inspirational Stories from America's Top Educators*. Adams Media, 2009.

About the Author

Aimee Ross is a nationally award-winning educator who has been a high school English teacher for the past twenty-five years and an aspiring writer for as long as she can remember. She completed her MFA in Creative Non-Fiction Writing at Ashland University in 2014, but she also dabbles in fiction and poetry. Her writing has been published on lifein10minutes.com and SixHens.com, as well as in *Beauty around the World: A Cultural Encyclopedia* (ABC-Clio, 2017); *Scars: An Anthology* (Et Alia Press, 2015); *Today I Made a Difference: A Collection of Inspirational Stories from America's Top Educators* (Adams Media, 2009); and *Teaching Tolerance* magazine. You can follow Aimee at aimeerossblog.wordpress.com.